GLOBAL HISTORY OF THE PRESENT
Series editor | Nicholas Guyatt

In the Global History of the Present series, historians address the upheavals in world history since 1989, as we have lurched from the Cold War to the War on Terror. Each book considers the unique story of an individual country or region, refuting grandiose claims of 'the end of history', and linking local narratives to international developments.

Lively and accessible, these books are ideal introductions to the contemporary politics and history of a diverse range of countries. By bringing a historical perspective to recent debates and events, from democracy and terrorism to nationalism and globalization, the series challenges assumptions about the past and the present.

Published

Thabit A. J. Abdullah, *Dictatorship, Imperialism and Chaos: Iraq since 1989*

Timothy Cheek, *Living with Freedom: China since 1989*

Alexander S. Dawson, *First World Dreams: Mexico since 1989*

Padraic Kenney, *The Burdens of Freedom: Eastern Europe since 1989*

Stephen Lovell, *Destination in Doubt: Russia since 1989*

Forthcoming

Alejandra Bronfman, *On the Move: The Caribbean since 1989*

James D. Le Sueur, *Between Terror and Democracy: Algeria since 1989*

Mark LeVine, *Impossible Peace: Israel/Palestine since 1989*

Hyung Gu Lynn, *Bipolar Orders: The Two Koreas since 1989*

Nivedita Menon and Aditya Nigam, *Power and Contestation: India since 1989*

Helena Pohlandt-McCormick, *What Have We Done? South Africa since 1989*

Nicholas Guyatt is assistant professor of history at Simon Fraser University in Canada.

About the author

Thabit A. J. Abdullah is associate professor in the Department of History at York University in Canada. His teaching and research focus on modern and medieval Iraq, the Indian Ocean and the Ottoman Empire. His recent publications include: *A Short History of Iraq: From 636 to the Present* (2003) and *Merchants, Mamluks and Murder: The Political Economy of Commerce in Eighteenth Century Basra* (2001).

Dictatorship, Imperialism and Chaos: Iraq since 1989

Thabit A. J. Abdullah

48-70:

1-How/why did Saddam attack Iraqi Kurds after the end of the Iran-Iraq War?

2-Why did Iraq invade Kuwait in 1990?

3-How did US policy contribute to both the March 1991 uprising & its failure? What was the effect on the position of the Shi'ah in Iraq?

Fernwood Publishing
NOVA SCOTIA

Zed Books
LONDON | NEW YORK

Dictatorship, Imperialism and Chaos: Iraq since 1989 was first published in 2006

Published in Canada by Fernwood Publishing Ltd, 32 Oceanvista Lane, Site 2A, Box 5, Black Point, Nova Scotia BOJ 1BO

<www.fernwoodbooks.ca>

Published in the rest of the world by Zed Books Ltd, 7 Cynthia Street, London N1 9JF, UK and Room 400, 175 Fifth Avenue, New York, NY 10010, USA

<www.zedbooks.co.uk>

Copyright © Thabit A. J. Abdullah, 2006

The right of Thabit A. J. Abdullah to be identified as the author of this work has been asserted by him in accordance with the Copyright, Designs and Patents Act, 1988.

Cover designed by Andrew Corbett
Set in OurTypeArnhem and Futura Bold by Ewan Smith, London
Index <ed.emery@britishlibrary.net>
Printed and bound in Malta by Gutenberg Press Ltd

Distributed in the USA exclusively by Palgrave Macmillan, a division of St Martin's Press, LLC, 175 Fifth Avenue, New York, NY 10010.

A catalogue record for this book is available from the British Library.
US CIP data are available from the Library of Congress.

Library and Archives Canada Cataloguing in Publication
Abdullah, Thabit
   Dictatorship, imperialism and chaos : Iraq since 1989 / Thabit A. J. Abdullah.
Includes bibliographical references and index.
ISBN 1-55266-204-7
   1. Iraq--History--1979-1991. 2. Iraq--History--1991-2003. 3. Iraq--History--2003-. I. Title.
DS79.76.A24 2006   956.7044'3   C2006-902635-1

ISBN 1 84277 786 6 | 978 1 84277 786 2 hb
ISBN 1 84277 787 4 | 978 1 84277 787 9 pb

Contents

Acknowledgments

The American invasion of Iraq in 2003 stirred up a host of contradictory feelings in many Iraqis. My wife and I, who were nervously watching the events from Syria, worried about American intentions and the eruption of uncontrollable forces. At the same time we rejoiced at the toppling of a brutal regime which had caused both our families terrible suffering. Three years on we are still struggling with these emotions. Overall, however, the first three years after the fall of Saddam Hussein have not yielded much cause for optimism. For this reason, the present book is not a happy read as it traces the process of the destruction of a country and a people. Given the present alignment of internal and external forces affecting Iraqi development, it seems unlikely that the country will reverse its fortunes in the near future.

I would like to thank the many fine people who assisted me in producing this work. Nicholas Guyatt, the editor of the Global History of the Present series, first contacted me and made several perceptive suggestions after reading the first draft. Janet Law copyedited the manuscript while Ellen McKinlay, Anna Hardman, Ewan Smith and Rosemary Taylorson did an excellent job managing the complicated administrative and editorial work. I would also like to thank my wife Samera, for her support, and my two children, Yasmine and Rami, for their patience and understanding.

to Professor Hanna Batatu

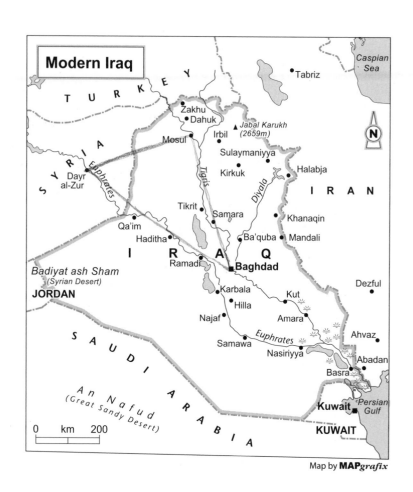

Modern Iraq

Caspian
Sea

T U R K E Y

Tabriz

Zakhu
Dahuk

Mosul
Irbil

▲ Jabal Karukh
(2659m)

Sulaymaniyya

S Y R I A

Kirkuk

Halabja

Dayr
al-Zur

Euphrates

Tigris

Diyala

I R A N

Tikrit

Samara

Khanaqin

Qa'im

Haditha

Ba'quba   Mandali

I R A Q

Ramadi

Baghdad

Badiyat ash Sham
(Syrian Desert)

JORDAN

Karbala

Hilla

Kut

Dezful

Najaf

Amara

Samawa

Euphrates

Nasiriyya

Ahvaz

Abadan

S A U D I   A R A B I A

Basra

An Nafud
(Great Sandy Desert)

Kuwait
Persian
Gulf

0   km   200

KUWAIT

N

Map by **MAP**grafix

Introduction

As a child growing up in Baghdad, I remember once how our school-teacher, hardly able to contain his enthusiasm, told us how much he admired the West for its "order." Many of us at the time thought it was a rather desperate attempt to dissuade the class from its normally rowdy behavior, but he did reflect a common feeling among our parents' generation. In hindsight, it seems that this betrayed a real fear of the latent disorder threatening a country wholly committed to rapidly catching up with the advanced industrial world. Iraq has paid a heavy price in its search for order, national integration and progress, and today it appears that our parents' worst nightmares are unfolding. This book tells the story of how modern Iraq, once one of the developing world's most progressive, wealthy and promising countries, fell into such decay that its very existence as a viable state is now questioned. Its main focus is the political and economic transformations, influenced by both internal and external factors, which in turn created deep fissures in Iraqi society.

The current lack of security, the burning of the National Library, and the continuing unsettled political situation, make research particularly challenging for any writer. On the other hand, the recent proliferation of a free and open Iraqi press and local NGOs have provided a new, rich source of information. This work takes an opposing view to the unfortunately fashionable talk of the "artificiality" of the Iraqi state.[1] According to this view, especially prevalent among current American ideologues, the ills of modern Iraq are the direct result of an "original sin" or "folly" committed by the English when they "lumped" together three distinct groups (Kurds, Shi'is and Sunnis) into a single state called Iraq. Hence, there is a lamentable need for a repressive ruler to keep them together. Without such a dictatorship, Christopher Catherwood argues, the country might very well fall apart: "[J]ust as the death of the local

strongman of Yugoslavia, Marshal Tito, led to the violent disintegra-
tion of his country and the bloodbath of the 1990s, so too might Iraq
now slide into chaos as its three very different component cultures
seek to coexist without the glue of tyranny to hold them together."[2]
This assumes that these "component cultures" are essentially un-
differentiated, immune to other overlapping identities, standing
above all other structures, unaffected by the constantly changing
economic and political context. It also assumes the passivity of the
Iraqi people in the face of British colonial designs. Catherwood,
echoing many writers, emphasizes the arbitrary nature of colonial
borders which are often simple straight lines. "But," he continues,
"groups of people do not live according to straight lines drawn with
a ruler. Ethnic boundaries are very complex things."[3] And yet no
one seems to be worried that, for example, the American–Canadian
border (half of which is a straight line along the 49th parallel) might
also raise charges of "artificiality." In fact, Iraq is no more artificial
than any other country with borders drawn as a result of a variety
of reasons including wars, treaties, compromises, backroom deals,
internal and external pressures, and plain chance. And Iraqis, like
any other people, have many overlapping identities which play different roles depending on the historical context and the problems
of the time. For sure, many people take seriously their religious
or ethnic identities and these have become especially pronounced
after the American invasion of 2003. But they also identify with their
kin, city, village, region, class, profession, political ideology, gender,
and generation. It is the contention of this work that the sectarian
divisions which today threaten the unity of the country are the result
not of the assertion of "essential" unchanging identities, but rather
of the unraveling of national structures as a result of forty years
of totalitarianism and terror, three savage wars, thirteen years of
a paralyzing embargo, and the complete decapitation of the state
through foreign invasion.

Looking at Iraq since 1989 one might be tempted to think that
the contemporary situation is simply a product of American intervention; but it is intimately tied to the rise of the modern state,
outlined in Chapter 1, which has deep roots in the past. To clarify
the historic roots of the present crisis, I have found it necessary to

devote nearly one-third of the book on the pre-1989 period. Far from being created arbitrarily, the land Iraq roughly now occupies has had a sense of economic and administrative unity going back centuries. But in the course of its evolution, state and society naturally changed, often having to break abruptly with past establishments. Such was the case in 1958 when a revolution destroyed many of the archaic vertical social structures and brought about reforms meant to accelerate a preexisting tendency toward national integration. In Chapter 2 I examine the nature of Ba'athist totalitarianism, Saddam's dictatorship, and the suppression of civil society. The result was that while the old traditional institutions were smashed by the revolution and its subsequent regimes, the dictatorship prevented the emergence of a civil society capable of filling the existing vacuum. This, along with the eight-year war with Iran, resulted in a devastated economy, a culture of violence and early signs of a shift toward increasing reliance on sub-national or primary associations. Chapter 3 looks at the tenuous two years of peace after the ceasefire with Iran and the subsequent disastrous invasion of Kuwait. The ensuing war decimated Iraq's infrastructure, initiated a mass uprising, and deepened social divisions. It also ushered in a decade of sanctions, dealt with in Chapter 4, which proved more destructive than anything the country had seen during the preceding wars. The sanctions eroded the base of the country's middle classes, accentuated social inequalities, gave rise to savage profiteering, and actually solidified the dictatorship's hold on power. Lastly, the American invasion and occupation are covered in Chapter 5. The events associated with the occupation are still unfolding but thus far it has led to the complete dismantling of the state apparatus without providing an effective alternative administration despite the best intentions of a number of Iraqi groups. This has encouraged lawlessness, corruption, violence, and further social fragmentation.

All of this took place within the broader context of the instability and confusion caused by the collapse of the socialist bloc and the end of an international configuration defined, to an extent, by the Cold War. Paradoxically, Iraq represents both the clearest and most ambiguous case of the Cold War's impact on the Middle East. Clearly, the collapse of the Soviet Union provided the United States with the opportunity to intervene directly in a region which was hotly contested by the two superpowers. But its impact is also somewhat ambiguous as the Middle East has, since the nineteenth century, repeatedly endured the attempts of Western powers to intervene, occupy and reshape the region. It is quite likely, then, that current American involvement will not usher in a qualitatively new age, but rather bring about a more chaotic and violent continuation of past developments.

1 | The rise of the modern state

The history of the state in the land of Iraq (ancient Mesopotamia) dates back to the dawn of human civilization around 3500 BCE. It was there that humans first established cities with laws regulating the increasingly complex relationships between the rulers and their subjects. By the end of the second millennium BCE, these city-states were gradually unified under several successive empires beginning with the Old Babylonian and ending with the Persian Sassanian. The most important determinant in the rise of the ancient state in Iraq was the existence of the two great rivers: the Tigris and the Euphrates. Not only were they the chief source of economic surplus but, more crucially, the two rivers also facilitated communication and social interaction which, in turn, led to interdependence and a degree of cultural affinity all along the river valleys. But topography rarely has a one-sided impact on social development since the two rivers were also the cause for divisions among the various peoples of Mesopotamia. In addition to competition between cities over water and land, limited land proprietorship gave rise to class tensions which, at times, broke out in violent peasant uprisings. Yet, perhaps the most unsettling impact on the cohesiveness of Mesopotamian society came from outside. Attracted by the great agricultural wealth of the land, or perhaps because of its central location, the country witnessed periodic waves of mass migrations. Whether peaceful or through violent conquests, these migrations constantly injected new social and cultural norms which were destabilizing but also brought about a sense of dynamism and progressive change to Iraqi society. For these reasons, Iraq remained, throughout its long history, a land inhabited by a highly heterogeneous population brought together by the two rivers.

Arab Islamic rule

In 636 CE, one such invasion was to prove decisive in the formation of the modern Iraqi identity. In that year, an army of Arab tribesmen, united by the new religion of Islam, defeated the main force of the Sassanian Empire and took the capital of Ctesiphon on the Tigris river.[1] In time, most Iraqis came to adopt both the Arabic language and the Islamic religion as their own, a condition that has remained unchanged in contemporary times. During the ninth and most of the tenth centuries, Iraq witnessed what can arguably be called a golden period as it became the center of a massive Muslim empire stretching from northern India and central Asia to Morocco and the Sudan. Under the effective rule of the first two centuries of the Abbasid dynasty (750–945), the country enjoyed great prosperity, cultural efflorescence, scientific enlightenment, and rapid demographic growth. In 762, the Caliph Abu Ja'far al-Mansur founded the new capital city of Baghdad which, at its height in 900, was the largest city in the world outside China. Baghdad added a new level of administrative and cultural cohesion to the land of Iraq. This period has remained firmly fixed in the modern Iraqi mentality as a source of pride and a reminder of the possibilities. Despite falling on hard times after the decline of the Abbasids in the late tenth century, the city continued to act as a center to which the rest of the country gravitated. This was true even after the highly destructive Mongol and Turkic conquests of the thirteen to fifteenth centuries.

During these turbulent centuries, known to Iraqis as the "Dark Period," a number of petty dynasties rose and fell over different parts of the country. Nevertheless, Baghdad maintained its position as the most important administrative center in the region with either real or at least nominal control over the other Iraqi towns. As the power of the central state waned, a number of protest movements rose to fill the vacuum. Normally, these movements sought to secure their legitimacy by challenging orthodox Sunni Islam, which had acted as the ideological base of the Baghdad Caliphate, by claiming allegiance to its rival Shi'i sect of Islam. Not until the mid-sixteenth century was this state of constant warfare, fragmentation, impoverishment, and steep demographic decline slowly reversed. During the course of the sixteenth century, the Middle East was reunified under the Ottoman and Safavid Empires. Though the two were implacable foes, often contesting each other on Iraqi soil, they nevertheless managed to bring relative order to the region after centuries of deprivation. The Safavids, who ruled much of Iraq from 1508 to 1534 and from 1623 to 1638, adhered to the Shi'i branch of Islam. Their founder, the young Shah Isma'il, believed that he was the instrument of God's will to purify Islam from within by imposing the Shi'i creed on conquered lands. For the Safavids, controlling Iraq was not only important because of its location, but, more crucially, because it contained the shrines of the most venerated Shi'i figures in the towns of Najaf, Karbala, Samarra, and Kazim. The Ottomans, on the other hand, were champions of Sunni Islam and sought legitimacy in their relentless expansion into non-Islamic Europe. Iraq, and Baghdad in particular, was valued as a defensive shield against their Safavid enemies, and because it was the seat of the great Abbasid caliphs whom the Ottoman sultans claimed to emulate.

Transformations under the Ottomans

Most of the time, the Ottomans governed Iraq through three provinces: Mosul, Baghdad, and Basra. The governor of Baghdad, however, was usually given powers over those of the other two provinces. Nevertheless, during their four-century rule of Iraq, the Ottomans had repeatedly to fight to keep the Safavids and their successors at bay. Over the course of this struggle the two belligerents signed a number of treaties in an effort to find lasting peace.[2] The treaties gradually delineated the eastern border of Iraq, though a number of sticking points remained unresolved well into the twentieth century, notably in the south around the area of Shatt al-'Arab. The Ottoman conflict with Iran also had serious repercussions on Iraq's Sunni–Shi'i relations. To justify waging war on fellow Muslims, each side had to declare the other's faith a heresy. While most local Sunni and Shi'i leaders counseled tolerance, sectarian tensions were heightened during this period. The most serious repressions took place shortly after the conquest of new territory where religious shrines or places of scholarship would be desecrated by partisans of the victorious power. This was more often done by the Safavids who destroyed such Sunni centers as the Abu Hanifa and Gaylani mosques, only to be rebuilt once the Ottomans resumed control. Ottoman measures against the Shi'i establishment took the form of freezing their leaders out of government positions. Over the long period of Ottoman rule, the Shi'i community adapted to this situation by turning inward. They established their own judicial courts, welfare institutions, and informal local governing bodies. Shi'i religious institutions gradually evolved a clearer hierarchy and an ability to function more autonomously than those of their Sunni counterparts, which continued to rely on government patronage. These divisions, however, were by no means absolute as many neighborhoods remained mixed and Sunni–Shi'i business partnerships were quite common. Likewise, Iraqi Shi'is tended to underline their Arab identity and different ideological leanings which separated them from their Iranian counterparts. The rivalry with Iran notwithstanding, Ottoman Iraq witnessed a gradual rise in population, the growth of towns, and an overall improvement in security. This, in turn, served to strengthen Iraqi elites, particularly the merchants, landholders, government officials, religious leaders, and tribal sheikhs. As their fortunes improved, these elites also became politically emboldened and brought greater vitality to a number of social institutions such as the many guilds, mystical orders, associations of descendants of the Prophet, neighborhood notables, and kinship groups. Although the borders between these groups were porous, on the whole they tended to be vertically organized.

By the mid-nineteenth century, the Middle East began to experience two interconnected transformations which, in many ways, have continued to fashion its development today. The first was a series of reforms and regulations intended to increase the power of the central state. For the Ottomans, who faced a growing danger from a resurgent Europe, this was a necessary change to strengthen the military by organizing the country's resources more efficiently. Ambitious reforms were announced in 1839, beginning with the creation of a modern army and taxation system, moving, in later years, to areas such as secular education and the establishment of a constitution in 1876. These reforms remained distant from the Iraqi provinces until 1869 when Midhat Pasha assumed the governorship of Baghdad. Under his enlightened leadership, Baghdad, as well as Basra and Mosul, modernized their bureaucracy, standardized administrative divisions, constructed new secular schools, put into effect laws encouraging private control of the land, and improved communications. The new Ottoman Sixth Army was stationed near Baghdad with a mandate to enforce the state's authority over all three provinces. The second transformation related to the region's gradual integration in the growing world economy dominated by European capital. Initially, this integration took place through a rapid increase in trade. This was particularly evident after the opening of the Suez Canal and the use of steamship navigation. Most of Iraq's foreign trade was with India, giving Britain the advantage in penetrating the Iraqi market.

The lucrative foreign trade coupled with state centralization brought about deep economic and social changes. Midhat Pasha's land laws and increasing trade with India transformed many of the tribal sheikhs into large landowners focusing on cash-crop production. This, in turn, reduced the tribesmen to sharecroppers, deepened class divisions, and weakened tribal solidarity. Some tribal sheikhs owed their positions to Ottoman favoritism and became strong supporters of government expansion into the countryside. Nomadic tribes were also brought closer to central control through policies aimed at their settlement. Settlement and class divisions tended to weaken many of the tribes though others remained defiant of state control well into the next century. In the cities, merchants, especially minorities, benefited by the increase in the import–export trade with Europe and India. Perhaps even more important was the introduction and spread of secular education. A new class of graduates emerged to threaten the position of the traditional elites. Valued for their modern education, they quickly came to dominate government posts and many of the professions, especially law. Minorities such as the Jews of Baghdad, found in secular education new opportunities for social advancement by enrolling to become lawyers, teachers, and doctors. Such steps resulted in the greater social, political, and economic integration of Iraq, but one cannot yet speak of an accompanying ideological nationalism.

Many of these changes accelerated after the 1908 Young Turk revolution in Istanbul which restored the constitution and expanded the reform movement. Recently there has been much talk of the novelty of elections in Iraq. Yet as far back as 1908 and again in 1912, elections were held for a new Ottoman parliament as well as local councils in Baghdad and other Iraqi cities. Though suffrage was quite limited, the elections still created a sense of political excitement with several, newly established, political parties participating. Shi'is were also drawn into many of these events, especially after the development of a strong constitutional movement in Iran in 1906. As Shi'i leaders followed closely the debates of their co-religionists in Iran, many wondered aloud whether such political reforms might work in their own country. The Young Turk period also saw the development of a budding Arab and Iraqi nationalism, mostly as a reaction to a perceived sense of ethnic discrimination. In keeping with their goal of creating stronger national unity, the Young Turk government adopted a policy of "Turkification" which essentially enforced Turkish as the single official language of the empire. All over the Arabic-speaking parts of the empire this policy was met with stiff resistance, often in the form of cultural clubs which glorified Arab history and language. In Iraq, opinions differed over the appropriate political response to the Young Turk challenge. While some expressed notions of Arab unity and secession, others focused on a specifically Iraqi autonomy. Prior to the First World War, a number of secret organizations appeared with specifically Arab nationalist goals. The most important was the Covenant Society which included several Iraqis, usually officers in the Ottoman army, many of whom would later play a leading role in the formation of the modern Iraqi state. Many of these clubs and political groups were secular with a particularly high participation of non-Muslims. Other groups, especially those that attracted elements from the Shi'i community, sought to define the nationalist project in Islamist terms by emphasizing the need to protect Islamic laws and culture.

This was also the time when foreign intervention intensified. In 1908, the region drew added international attention with the discovery of oil in southern Iran, not far from the Iraqi border. Britain was the most interested country, especially after the conversion of its naval fleet from coal to oil fuel. Oil, the region's strategic location, and the growing political crisis in Europe all encouraged an intense rivalry among several European powers including Britain, Germany, Russia, and France. In 1912, a British-dominated consortium, the Turkish Petroleum Company, was established in the hopes that oil would be found in Iraq. Britain also tried to sabotage an earlier Ottoman–German agreement to construct the so-called Berlin-to-Baghdad railway. Later, Britain agreed to drop its objections to this line provided it could control the construction and management of the southern part connecting Baghdad to the Persian Gulf.

War and the formation of the modern state

It took the Ottomans several months before they finally decided to throw their full weight behind the German war effort in 1914. Scarcely a day after the Ottoman entry into the war, British forces landed in Basra, starting one of the most grueling campaigns of the war. Initially, the British sought to take only Basra and its hinterland to secure its oil operations in Iran and its trade links with India. Yet the ease with which they accomplished this task and the urging of a number of important Iraqi figures to move on Baghdad changed their thinking. After some serious setbacks and nearly 100,000 casualties, the British army entered Baghdad in 1917 and Mosul in 1918. During the war, the British publicly promised independence to the Arabs on several occasions. General Stanley Maude, leader of the British army in Iraq, repeated this line when he famously declared: "Our armies do not come into your cities and lands as conquerors or enemies, but as liberators." At the same time, however, they secretly agreed to divide their control of the Fertile Crescent with the French. According to the so-called Sykes–Picot Agreement of 1916, France would receive the lands which later formed Syria and Lebanon, while Britain would get Iraq, Jordan and Palestine. After the war, the newly established League of Nations recognized the British occupation of Iraq as a "Mandate." The country was to remain under British control "until such time as ... [it is] able to stand alone." This was a bitter blow to the country's embryonic national leadership which had hoped for a rapid move to independence.

Other sources of tension developed as a result of the ongoing economic and social changes. Chief among these was the steady march of state centralization. Under British control this process continued

but appeared even less coherent than it had been under the Ottomans. To win over some local support, the British granted tribal
leaders greater administrative powers through the Tribal Criminal
and Civil Disputes Regulations of 1916. According to this law, which
was later installed in the constitution, tribal sheikhs were allowed to
collect taxes, administer, police, and uphold customary tribal law, in
their own recognized territories. At the same time, however, other
aspects of centralization, such as the appointment of tribal sheikhs,
decisions concerning major development projects, the distribution
of funds, control over water rights, and stricter control over the
towns, received greater attention. These two factors – nationalist
disillusionment with British policies and fears of state centralization
– combined to create a strong resistance movement which would
eventually succeed in establishing the modern state of Iraq.

Rebellion and independence

In 1920, the tribes of the mid-Euphrates region rebelled in opposition to state encroachment. Nationalists in Baghdad and religious
leaders in Najaf and Karbala quickly moved to lend the rebellion
ideological direction. It took the British four months to put the
rebellion down after it had spread to various parts of the country
including the Kurdish north. Over 10,000 Iraqis were killed in the
process. While the rebellion failed to evict the British, it did leave
a prominent mark in two ways. First, by bringing together various
communities (albeit briefly) in a common fight under specifically
Iraqi patriotic slogans, it enhanced national consciousness and
broadened the ideological appeal of the independence movement.
Notions of national unity were amplified by poets such as Muhammad al-'Ubaydi who wrote:

> Do not talk of Ja'fari or Hanafi
> do not talk of Shafi'i or Zaydi
> for the shari'a of Muhammad has united us
> and it rejects the Western mandate.[3]

Second, the uprising forced the British to alter their policy of
direct control. After some consideration, they opted for the establishment of an independent Iraqi state tied to Britain through treaties

ensuring British interests. This, of course, meant that the emerging state would suffer from serious limitations to its independence, a condition guaranteeing a continuation of tensions. Nevertheless, in 1921, Faisal, the son of Sharif Hussein of Mecca and leader of the Arab Revolt against the Ottomans, was crowned Iraq's first king. At that time, the country's 2.5–3 million people were still deeply divided along religious, ethnic, linguistic, regional, and tribal lines. About 55 percent were Arab Shi'is inhabiting the regions south of Baghdad; 20 percent were Arab Sunnis occupying the areas north of Baghdad; 20 percent were Sunni Kurds in the northern part of the country along the Turkish and Iranian borders; and the balance was made up of various Christian sects, Jews, Yazidis, Mandaeans, and others. The Kurds were the most distinct of all the non-Arab communities and represented the greatest challenge to national integration. In trying to manage the new country, colonial leaders often assumed that ethnic identities superseded all others when, in fact, issues of economic well-being tended to play the decisive role. A good example of this can be seen with respect to the so-called Mosul question. Soon after the end of the war, Turkey, now reconstituted as a vibrant republic, officially claimed the northern part of Iraq. It argued that technically Mosul was still part of Turkey since the British seized much of this territory after the signing of the armistice. The British, on the other hand, argued that Mosul was historically tied to Baghdad and that the new state of Iraq would lose its viability without its northern half. A commission was sent to the territory by the newly established League of Nations. The investigators had originally assumed that their task would be a simple one and that ethnic identities would ultimately decide political loyalties. What they discovered instead was a far more complex picture with economic considerations often trumping others: "Arabs who thought commerce was better before the war spoke in favour of Turkey. Turks who believed the countryside was more secure than previously were in favour of continued British control. Many Turks would have favoured union with Turkey, but abhorred the new [republican] government."[4]

In the end, the commission ruled in favor of Iraq while noting that Kurdish rights must be respected. These were defined as the right to appointment to the administrative, judicial, and educational institutions of the province, and the use of Kurdish as an official language.

In terms of the economy, literacy, or general education, Iraq as a whole was one of the most backward regions of the old Ottoman Empire. None of the borders was clearly demarcated and the only protection against foreign, especially Turkish and Iranian, incursions was the British army. This fact was actually driven home more than once whenever Faisal failed to satisfy British demands. In 1921, Winston Churchill, then the Secretary of State for the Colonies, wrote to the Prime Minister urging a strong policy on Iraq:

> I think we should now put definitely, not only to Feisal but also to the [Iraqi] Constituent Assembly, the position that unless they actually beg us to stay on our own terms in regard to efficient control, we shall actually evacuate beyond the close of the financial year. I would put this issue in the most brutal way, and if they are not prepared to urge us to stay and co-operate in every manner I would actually clear out. That at any rate would be a solution. Whether we should clear out of the country altogether or hold onto a portion of the Basra vilayet [or province] is a minor issue requiring special study.[5]

Politically, the new country was to be a constitutional monarchy and, in 1925, a new constitution was adopted. The constitution notwithstanding, there were, in fact, three centers of power: the king, parliament, and the British, who still had advisers and a considerable military presence. Large landowners, mainly Sunni Arabs who had been close to Faysal during his Arab Revolt, dominated the important government posts. While political life under the monarchy was anything but a stable democracy, the press and a number of opposition parties did enjoy limited freedoms, which they employed with considerable success. Most political parties were still organized around important personalities or elite families rather than clearly formulated ideals, but this would change with time. Throughout the nearly six decades of monarchic rule, the same figures (such as the indefatigable Nuri al-Sa'id) tended to occupy the positions of power. Still, two ideological currents began slowly to emerge, discernible

in both state-sponsored and opposition parties. One current tended
to emphasize the country's regional links, arguing that the road to
genuine sovereignty and prosperity must pass through Arab unity.
This argument found support particularly among the Arab Sunni
middle classes who could easily identify with the broader Sunni Arab
world. The other current argued that solving the country's internal
social and economic problems must take priority over broader
nationalist aspirations. In the Kurdish areas, a unified political elite
struggled to emerge but one tribal chieftain, Mahmud Barazanchi,
made repeated claims for self-rule until he was defeated and his
movement suppressed in the 1930s.

The first decade after the British occupation was spent developing the new institutions of government, negotiating the country's
borders with its neighbors, and working out Iraq's exact relationship
with Britain. In 1930, the Anglo-Iraqi Treaty was signed, according
to which the country would receive its independence provided it
agreed to British control or influence over Iraq's foreign policy and
military. Britain also gained the right to maintain two airbases near
Baghdad and Basra. In other agreements, Britain secured complete
control over Iraq's oil operations through the British-dominated
Iraqi Petroleum Company, a consortium of several companies. Iraqi
nationalists condemned the treaty as a capitulation to colonialism,
while pro-government leaders argued that this was but a first step
toward complete independence. Two years later, Iraq gained its
formal independence and was admitted to the League of Nations
as a sovereign state. In this manner the struggle against British
domination was one of the most important factors defining Iraqi
nationalism.

The monarchy 1932-58 = social & economic development, but no social base of support

Between 1932 and 1958 the monarchy achieved much in the way
of social and economic development but failed spectacularly in
building a social base of support. For sure, the challenges were not
light and, in many ways, the problems of nation-building facing the
young country were not completely different from those which still
plague it today. Internally, as mentioned earlier, Iraqis were divided
along various communal, or "sub-national," lines. Such divisions

ethnic divisions

were not helped by continued Arab Sunni dominance over state institutions. Regionally, the surrounding countries exerted strong influence upon specific communities in hopes of furthering their own aspirations. Most of the leading Shiʻi figures of Najaf, Karbala and Kazim had ties with their counterparts in Iran; many Arab Sunni leaders looked toward unity with Syria; and Turkey maintained its influence over elements within the Turkoman and Kurdish communities. Large tribal confederations paid little attention to the newly drawn or newly enforced borders which threatened to separate them from kinsmen or interrupt centuries-old migration routes. Further afield, a number of global powers vied to increase their hegemony over a country with strategic location and rich resources. Britain was clearly in an advantageous position early on, but after the end of the Second World War and the onset of the Cold War, both the United States and the Soviet Union came to play more prominent roles.

Throughout the period of the monarchy a number of developments were to sow the seeds for the turbulent political changes of the 1960s. Landed interests solidified their semi-feudal status through such draconian measures as the Rights and Duties of Cultivators Law of 1933 and the Lazma Law of 1952, both of which effectively bound the peasants to the land and gave landowners exemption from most taxes. Though such laws were amended or even flouted, they remained a symbol of the country's backwardness and an obstacle to industrial development and national integration. By 1958, about 80 percent of the peasants were landless, and only 1.7 percent of landowners owned over 63 percent of all cultivated land. Burdened by such a structure, Iraq's peasantry was regarded as among the world's most destitute with a life expectancy of no more than thirty-five to thirty-nine years. In order to promote national integration and achieve greater independence from Britain, King Faisal and his successors constantly increased the size and strength of the Iraqi army. In 1934, the law of general conscription was widely supported by the urban elite. Most of the new officers, who hailed from middle-level Sunni backgrounds, held strong nationalist views and deeply resented foreign controls. The growing crisis in Palestine and Britain's perceived role in supporting the Zionist movement further inflamed feelings. A harbinger of things to come appeared in 1936 when General Bakr Sidqi led a coup which replaced one cabinet with another and placed the army in the role of political arbitrator. In 1941, the army took on the more ambitious step of challenging the British presence by attempting to establish ties with the Axis powers. Though this last coup failed and ultimately had the opposite effect on the enfeebled monarchy, it did enjoy widespread support in the country.

Another important development was the rapid extension of education at all levels. This, however, had contradictory effects. On the one hand, the state could justifiably claim credit for reducing illiteracy and establishing impressive colleges which were putting out an increasing number of professionals in all fields. On the other hand, it also produced a new generation with high expectations and an ability to articulate its demands and organize its activities. They often provided the leadership for new ideological political parties, such as the Iraqi Communist Party, the National Democratic Party and the Independence Party, which were particularly critical of the monarchy and continued British tutelage. The Iraqi Communist Party, formed in 1932, had, by the late 1950s, grown to become the largest and best-organized political organization in the country. Other than opposing the government, it was noted for its ability to form non-governmental institutions such as unions for labor, women, students, youth, artists, and others. While the party eventually failed to seize power, it nevertheless played a crucial role in the development of civil society and a broad political awareness among ordinary Iraqis. Other groups also contributed to the embryonic development of modern horizontally-based social institutions.

Urban tension was augmented by a tidal-wave of rural migrants which saw Baghdad grow eight-fold between 1919 and 1960. These rural migrants, impoverished, illiterate, and alienated from their new surroundings, were easily moved to action by the opposition parties. Some of these migrants found their way into the newly developing industrial working class which constantly struggled for the right to form unions and improve its working conditions. To counter resentment and solidify the central government, the monarchy renegotiated its oil arrangements with the Iraqi Petroleum Company. In 1952, it greatly increased its oil revenues with a new 50:50 profit-sharing

socielly econ. agreement. This, plus the expansion of the country's export facilities,
based on al. transformed the Iraqi economy from one based chiefly on agricul-
under foreign tural exports to one dependent on oil but still largely controlled by
control foreign interests. By 1958, a full 62 percent of state revenues came
from oil. Politically, this meant that the state became less beholden
no revenue (tax) to any of the country's social classes since most of its income was
dependence now derived from sources other than taxation. While this did give the
on sigle state greater freedom of action, it also tended to increase its aliena-
groups in society tion from society. Quantity of output and pricing remained firmly in
pricing/production the hands of the foreign consortium guaranteeing a continuous state
under foreign of friction with the Iraqi government for decades to come.
control

The 1950s saw several internal and external factors combining
to undermine the power of the monarchy and usher in a decade
50s = violent of violent revolutionary change. The atmosphere of the Cold War
rev. change tended to sharpen internal antagonisms with the communists and
Arab nationalists leading the opposition while the monarchy sought
to bind the country ever tighter to the West. In 1956, Iraq became a
56 = Baghdad founding member of the so-called Baghdad Pact. Sponsored by the
Pact = v. soviet United States and Britain, this regional alliance was seen as a key
influence link in the global effort to contain Soviet influence. Regionally, the
defeat of the Arab armies (including the Iraqi army) in Palestine
in 1948, followed by the 1952 Revolution in Egypt, and the instal-
ling of a radical government in Iran that same year, combined to
agitate for revolutionary change at home. The charismatic Nasser
of Egypt had a strong impact on Arab society in general and Iraq in
particular with his calls for overthrowing the "corrupt" monarchies,
the elimination of foreign hegemony and the enactment of social
welfare policies. As the voice of the opposition grew louder, the
monarchy, led by the regent 'Abdul-Ilah and the Prime Minister Nuri
al-Sa'id, responded with rigged elections and increasing repression.
Demonstrations, strikes, clashes, and executions were repeated in
1948, 1952 and 1956.

Revolution and reform

The 1950s and 1960s were decades of revolutionary change
throughout the Middle East and much of the world. The post-Second
World War order was being challenged by a variety of nationalist

and socialist movements directed chiefly against Western capitalist hegemony. In this sense, the revolutionary period which swept through Iraq was no different. What was, to a degree, more specific to Iraq was the mechanism of change which in turn affected the resultant dynamics. Outwardly, the causes for change were obvious: foreign control of the oil resources, the presence of British military bases, the intolerable situation in the countryside, a demand for greater solidarity with Palestine and Egypt, and a desire to remain neutral in the Cold War. But behind such demands was the subtle push for national integration. Demands such as greater educational opportunities, land reform, employment, labor and women's rights, more Shi'i participation in the centers of power, and the recognition of Kurdish national rights, all combined to promote national integration. Many political parties struggled to prepare the ground ideologically for change. But it was the army, the strongest national institution, which eventually carried out the *coup de grâce*.

[handwritten margin note: goal = national integration]

On the morning of July 14, 1958, a section of the army led by General 'Abdul-Karim Qasim and Colonel 'Abdul-Salam 'Arif rapidly secured the major centers of power in Baghdad. As the news spread, large demonstrations, often led by the Communist Party, took to the streets in support of the coup. In the following days a number of the leading figures associated with the monarchy would be killed, and various symbols of the old regime and their foreign backers destroyed. Significantly, the mass demonstrations never took on a communal or sectarian form. Even in some parts of the countryside, where sub-national identities were much stronger, considerations of class predominated with peasants tending to target the estates of the landowners and big tribal sheikhs. The government which Qasim formed and the reforms it undertook reflected this populist, anti-imperialist mood and quickly transformed Iraqi society and politics in fundamental ways. This transformation, however, was anything but smooth. For while the leaders of the coup agreed on the need to establish a republic and secure the country's political and economic independence, deep fissures divided them over the means and extent of such goals.

[handwritten margin note: July 14, '58 = military coup]

[handwritten margin note: allegiances along class lines]

[handwritten margin note: new regime = tried to channel populist anti-imperial mood]

The new regime was republican in form and dominated by the military leaders of the revolution, especially Qasim who became prime minister. The exact nature of the republic was to be outlined by a new democratic constitution after the old regime was completely "rooted out" – a process that could have taken several years and various reforms. Qasim's reforms tended toward a national-liberal rather than a radical or socialist policy. In general, these reforms were well received by the urban bourgeoisie and broad sections of the lower classes. In the tense atmosphere of the Cold War and Nasser's ambitious Middle East policy, however, they raised alarms from Cairo to Washington. Internally, a mild land reform was initiated to alleviate the problem of landlessness and to destroy the political power of the landlords. Qasim repeatedly stated that this was not an attack upon the wealthy but an attempt to alleviate the plight of the poor:

new constitution

attempt to alleviate poverty

> We will not persecute landlords or treat them unjustly. We will only awaken their conscience towards the sons of this people, and they will march alongside the caravan of liberation and equality. [...] Our aim is to eradicate greed. [...] The small must respect the big and the big must cherish the small, so that we may form one unit serving one aim.[6]

tribal laws / legal standing of women

It also did away with tribal laws, improved the legal position of women, relaxed regulations limiting the growth of civil society institutions, and appointed the Arab world's first woman minister. The temporary constitution of the new Republic for the first time acknowledged that Iraq was a bi-national state of Arabs and Kurds. Reforms affecting international relations included the withdrawal from the Baghdad Pact and the adoption of a policy of non-alignment, the eviction of British troops, and the establishment of full diplomatic and economic relations with the socialist bloc. More importantly, Qasim passed a law limiting the control of the Iraqi Petroleum Company and started negotiations over an increased share of the oil profits. In 1960, Iraq became a founding member of an oil producers' association later named the Organization of Petroleum Exporting Countries (OPEC).

no more Baghdad Pact, eviction of British, relations w/Soviet Union

limited control of Iraqi Petrol. Company

While these and other reforms were extremely popular in Iraq, they veiled a tendency toward personal rule on the part of Qasim and a number of his associates (notably 'Arif) which grew more confrontational with each internal or external obstacle. More than any other,

[margin note: question of Arab unity = point of contention]

the issue which brought the various disagreements into sharp focus was the question of Arab unity as championed by Egypt's Nasser. In 1958, Egypt and Syria merged to create the United Arab Republic, and it was hoped that revolutionary Iraq would immediately join. Qasim refused and argued for a more loosely-formed confederation. The stand-off gave the anti-Qasim forces a strong regional ally in the form of Nasser who did not shrink from hatching one plot after another to bring the so-called Arab nationalists to power in Iraq. Behind the plethora of slogans and heightened polemics, the tensions in post-revolutionary Iraq betrayed more profound differences. Qasim's reforms offended many established classes, chiefly the landed interests and certain conservative groups who feared his liberal and secular bias. His confrontation with Britain and the United States over oil and non-alignment was greatly intensified when he made an ill-timed claim over Kuwait. Yet, while the constellation of forces aligned against him on the right grew, he was unwilling to seek allies on the left. He regarded the communists with deep suspicion and his refusal to draw Iraq closer to the socialist bloc served only to increase his international isolation. His rejection of Pan-Arabism also illustrates the manner in which Iraqi nationalism was constantly pulled in various directions by forces emphasizing different loyalties. In addition to the local affiliations of a sub-national type, Pan-Arabism represented the other side of the spectrum; a sort of "extra-national" or regional identity. In this manner, Iraqi nation-building, like that of other countries, must be seen as a process in which various forces constantly struggled to find a balance or compromise between competing identities which very often went well beyond the simple notion of Kurds, Sunnis, and Shi'is.

[margin notes: '58 = United Arab Republic (Egypt + Syria) / (pro-UAR feeling in Iraq v. Quasim); alienating landed class Britain & US; no allies on the left; Iraqi nationali not set in sto]

Reaction

Faced with such a situation it was only a matter of time before Qasim was overthrown in the military coup of 1963. Colonel 'Arif, Qasim's one-time ally, a staunch conservative, and supporter of Nasser, formed an alliance with the small but rapidly growing Arab Ba'ath (or Resurrection) Socialist Party. Founded in neighboring Syria in 1944, the Ba'ath Party adhered to a vague ideology of "Nationalist Socialism" and fashioned itself as the vanguard Pan-

[margin note: '63 = coup v. Quasim, by pro-UAR forces]

[bottom note: Arab Ba'ath Party = Arab Resurrection Party ("Nationalist Socialism")]

Arab political organization whose main goals were the unity of the Arab peoples (from Morocco to Iraq), and the end of all forms of foreign hegemony. It opposed both the Arab monarchies and the communists because of their "foreign" ties. The coup inaugurated several days of mass killings and arrests of Qasim and his supporters, but most of the brutality was reserved for the communists. The Ba'ath's main instrument of slaughter were the National Guards, a paramilitary group roughly organized along fascist lines. Young, immature, and often the "toughs" of their neighborhoods, they were quick to resort to violence. Though hard evidence is still lacking, accusations that the putschists were aided by American and French intelligence cannot be dismissed given the climate of the Cold War at the time and the similarity with events in Iran, Latin America and elsewhere which were later proved to have had CIA backing. Still, the atrocities appeared to have been too much even for some of the coup leaders themselves. Several months after the takeover, 'Arif removed the Ba'athists and relaxed the government's grip but without ending the state of emergency.

On many levels 'Arif's (and his brother's) regime was a typical form of military rule backed by a myriad of Arab nationalist groups. The 'Arif brothers ruled for five years and were more notable for their failures than for their accomplishments. Having come to power with the promise of immediate unity with Nasser's Egypt they succeeded in adopting only the same flag and national anthem but little else. Nasser's influence was felt, however, in a number of internal reforms such as the adoption of a single political party, the Arab Socialist Union, widespread nationalizations and a new land reform. The nationalizations represented the clearest departure from Qasim's approach since it dealt a blow to the urban bourgeoisie. Most of the nationalized industries were placed under the management of select military commanders. 'Arif had also promised the Kurdish leadership, notably the veteran Mullah Mustafa al-Barzani, a favorable settlement of their national demands. Instead, talks broke down and armed conflict erupted in the Kurdish north which lasted, with few interruptions, until the American invasion of 2003. 'Arif's inability to secure popular support, added to his own parochial outlook, led him to appoint members of his family and tribe to leading posts.

Many of the military and political leaders promoted by 'Arif came from the tribal or rural areas of the so-called Arab Sunni Triangle stretching roughly from Baghdad north to Mosul and west to the Syrian boarder. Unlike their counterparts in the south, the tribes of these regions were not afflicted by deep class divisions and the gap between rich and poor remained relatively limited. Thus, notions of tribal solidarity rang particularly loud there, allowing 'Arif and his other associates to make full use of them. During the monarchy, thousands of ambitious youths from these areas joined the army and police in a bid to escape the poverty of the villages. As one of the few opportunities available to them, the army allowed many to move up the ranks and eventually to hold prominent posts.

[handwritten margin notes: appt. people from area where tribal allegiance > class division; army = meritocratic]

While the 'Arif regime never managed to achieve stability, especially during its last two years, the various opposition groups, including the communists and Kurdish nationalists, had regrouped and increased their activities. Divisions within the leadership deepened, especially after the death of the charismatic 'Abdul-Salam 'Arif and the coming to power of his rather weak younger brother. Ideologically, the regime's Nasserist leaning failed to convince, given their hesitation to accept Nasser's leadership. The final blow to its prestige came with the resounding defeat of the Arab armies in the 1967 war with Israel. Though Iraq hardly played a role in that conflict, the regime's critics, especially from the Arab nationalist camp, accused it of negligence and the betrayal of Arab solidarity. Chief among these critics was the reorganized Ba'ath Party now firmly under the leadership of Ahmad Hasan al-Bakr, a senior military officer, and a young civilian by the name of Saddam Hussein.

[handwritten margin notes: 'Arif weakened by failure to accept Nasser's leadership, Kurdish demands]

Ba'athist totalitarianism

[handwritten: — Saddam Hussein]

In 1968, the Ba'ath Party, along with a number of malcontent army officers, seized power for a second time. Though they were driven from power by 'Arif, Ba'athists never suffered the type of severe repression which was reserved for the communists. During the five years leading up to its second coup, the Ba'ath was reorganized under a new leadership hailing mostly from the rural areas around Tikrit. Still, the party, with its emphasis on Arab unity, did not overtly discriminate between Sunnis and Shi'is during its early period in power.

[handwritten: Not v. Sunni yet (emphasis on unity)]

The party's rank and file was primarily Shi'i and even contained Kurds and Christians. The post of Minister of Interior, for example, was initially entrusted to the Shi'i Nazim Kazar. While this ministry would later become a Sunni monopoly, non-Sunni elements, such as the Shi'i Sa'dun Hammadi and the Christian Tariq 'Aziz, remained prominent in some high posts. Having gone through power struggles and splits, the new leadership placed a premium on internal party control. To this end they entrusted Saddam Hussein with forming an internal security service which eventually became his personal power base within the party. A few days after securing their hold, the Ba'ath established a full monopoly on power. The next ten years would see the Ba'ath finally settling the debate over the exact nature of the post-monarchy state. In the decade following the 1958 Revolution, the most important pillars of the old monarchy were effectively destroyed. These included the royal family, parliament, the powerful rural landowning classes, and the various instruments of British influence. It was never fully clear, however, what was going to replace them. The Ba'athists energetically set out to build a totalitarian state with a republican veneer.

Totalitarianism had been a growing threat in Iraq well before the Ba'ath seizure of power. Throughout the 1950s and 1960s Iraq, as did many Third World countries, witnessed the growing popularity of a "development ethos" which argued that economic development was the key to social justice. To guard against the control of foreign capitalists or local "compradors," and to ensure that investments would be concentrated in the areas of general need rather than individual profit, development had to be directed by a nationalist state. The land reform and nationalizations of Qasim and 'Arif placed great resources in the hands of the state and allowed it to reward its supporters and transform a growing number of the population into employees of the state. Not that the state was against capitalist development as such; rather, its fear of foreign domination, as under the monarchy, encouraged the idea of a strong role for the state as a sort of "incubator" for domestic capital. A second factor was the accompanying rise of a "revolutionary ethos," especially after the fall of the monarchy. In the ensuing battles against the old regime and within the revolutionary groups themselves, exacerbated by additional tensions from the Arab–Israeli conflict and the Cold War, the differences between domestic and foreign enemies tended to be blurred. Calls for greater "national vigilance," the closing of ranks and defense preparation, were widely applauded even by the democratic-minded. Notions of representative government and a new republican constitution were pushed to the background not simply through repression but also by the anti-imperialist mind-set of the time. Democracy was equated with "bourgeois" institutions imposed by the imperialist West. Slogans aside, well before the Ba'ath came to monopolize power, the internal security services, the army, and the general culture of repression and violence were all on the rise.

State expansion took on a qualitative leap with the dramatic rise in oil prices soon after the Ba'athist takeover. In 1972, the Ba'athist leadership took a daring and widely popular step by fully nationalizing the petroleum industry. Using the 1973 Arab–Israeli war as an excuse, Iraq, along with other OPEC countries, decreased production, driving prices up by 380 percent. Between 1972 and 1980, Iraq's oil revenues jumped from $575 million to $26,500 million (see Table 1.1). By the end of the decade, oil accounted for over 60 percent of Iraq's GDP and 95 percent of its foreign currency earnings. Table 1.1 illustrates the rapid growth of oil revenues in the 1970s.

TABLE 1.1 Oil production and revenues, 1972–80

Year	Crude oil production (millions of metric tonnes)	Oil revenue (US $ millions)
1972	72.1	575
1973	99.0	1,900
1974	96.7	6,000
1975	111.0	8,000
1976	118.8	8,500
1977	115.2	9,500
1978	125.7	11,600
1979	170.6	21,200
1980	130.2	26,500

Source: C. Whittleton, "Oil and the Iraqi Economy," in CARDRI, *Saddam's Iraq*, p. 65.

Academics have recently paid a great deal of attention to the nature of states that depend on revenue, such as oil, gained from sources other than taxation. The term usually applied here is "rentier" or "allocation" states. Such states are not accountable to a broad social base of support yet are still capable of wielding unrivaled economic, hence political, power. From 1958 to 1977, the number of state employees grew from 20,000 to 580,000 with an additional 230,000 in the armed forces and 200,000 pensioners. This meant that as much as 40 percent of households were directly dependent on the state for their livelihood. It is not too difficult to see how this situation, especially when factoring in the radical nationalist ideology of the Ba'ath, could easily lead to totalitarianism. Gradually, all unions, public establishments, charitable organizations and sports clubs were brought under state control. Nationalizations broadened to include all schools and even most religious establishments. Political loyalty, and even membership of the Ba'ath Party, rather than technical ability, came to determine appointments to the leading industrial or educational institutions. Of special concern to the Ba'ath was the nature of general education. Early on, a party document underscored the problem in this manner:

> The next five years must be devoted to building an educational system compatible with the principles and aims of the Party and the Revolution. [...] New syllabuses must at once be prepared for every level from nursery school to university, inspired by the principles of the Party and the Revolution. [...] Reactionary bourgeois and liberal ideas and trends in the syllabus and the educational institutions must be rooted out. The new generation must be immunized against ideologies and cultures conflicting with our Arab nation's basic aspirations and its aims for unity, liberty and socialism.[7]

The chief goal of education had little to do with developing technical know-how or a critical worldview, rather it was supposed to instill a "love of order," an eagerness to do battle, and a strong emphasis on notions of masculinity and honor. In one speech before becoming president, Saddam Hussein explained:

> the student who gets used to working through the many details and types of orders, for this reason as well as others, will, when necessity

a broad and ruthless military offensive in the north broke the back of the Kurdish resistance and drove its leadership into exile. This was followed in 1978 and 1979 with an attack on the Communist Party which was still recovering from its suppression under the 'Arif regime. While it continues to survive today, collaboration with the Ba'ath, followed by another wave of violent repression, drove its numerous supporters to despair and greatly reduced its subsequent impact. The Ba'ath's predisposition to violence and widespread terror was present from its early formative period. As far back as 1943, Michel 'Aflaq, the founder and chief ideologue of the party, wrote: "in this struggle [for Arab unity] we retain our love for all. When we are cruel to others, we know that our cruelty is in order to bring them back to their true selves, of which they are ignorant."[12]

Not long after their seizure of power in 1968, the new regime made a clear statement of intent when it staged a grisly spectacle in the main public square of Baghdad. Carried on Iraqi television for all to see, a number of supposed "spies" were beaten and hanged in front of a huge crowd with one official declaring that this was "only the beginning." Screaming at the top of his voice he went on to say: "The great and immortal squares of Iraq shall be filled up with corpses of traitors and spies! Just wait!"[13] By the end of the decade police terror had become common with reports of torture, including rape, widespread. The file of one "interrogator" who worked for the security services listed his official activity as "violation of women's honour."[14] Several draconian laws were passed holding whole families (up to "fourth degree" of relationship) of "conspirators" responsible for their relative's crimes. Ba'thist terror became so widespread that it even included its own ranks. An article of the Iraqi Penal Code included in the late 1970s stipulates the death penalty for:

- Concealment by Ba'ath Party members of their former political affiliations.
- Joining the Ba'ath Party while maintaining contact with another political party or organization.
- Leaving the Ba'ath Party and joining another party.
- Persuading a Ba'ath Party member to leave the Ba'ath Party.[15]

Regionally, the Ba'ath developed a more radical and uncompromising approach to the Arab–Israeli conflict which constantly provided it with the rationale to launch new waves of repression against supposed "collaborators." After the 1973 October War, Iraq led the way in forming a Rejectionist Front to confront the new peace efforts and in 1978 it again assumed center stage in its opposition to the Egyptian–Israeli Peace Treaty. Throughout these events, Iraq stressed its natural right to assume the role of the leader of the Arab world as a whole. Internationally, Iraq signed a Treaty of Friendship and cooperation with the USSR and rapidly increased its economic and military ties with the socialist bloc. This, however, was not done at the expense of its ties with the West, especially with France, which continued to be strong. And while diplomatic relations with the United States had been suspended after the 1967 Arab–Israeli War, commercial ties remained strong with trade being fifteen times greater in 1975 than it was in 1965.

By the end of the 1970s, the Ba'ath seemed completely in control of the country. Through a combination of ruthlessness, widespread terror, indoctrination, and a general sense of real material progress, it had been able either to eliminate or coopt its main competitors. In many ways, the Ba'ath picked up where the 1958 Revolution had left off. The revolution's primary achievement was the dismantling of traditional structures such as tribal laws and the privileged position of notable families. But rather than nurturing the development of a modern civil society that could fill the gap left by traditional structures, the Ba'ath, assisted by the almost unlimited oil revenues, actively suppressed its development. This, in turn, affected the process of national integration. Ever since the establishment of the modern state of Iraq, the country had been progressing, with difficulty, toward greater national integration. This was achieved not only on the level of the ruling elite and the state but also on the level of the opposition. Up to the mid-1960s, the main opposition, the communists, drew their support from various communities with their emphasis on working-class solidarity and a platform with a clear national non-sectarian focus. This progress received a setback after the 1963 coup which brought to the helm elements whose support base lay primarily among the Sunni rural communities just to the north and west of Baghdad. Ideologically, they emphasized Arab nationalism, which alienated the Kurds, and, to a lesser extent, the Shi'is. During the last two decades of Ba'athist rule, sectarian tendencies would deepen as the regime began to take bold, and ultimately disastrous, moves to extend its regional ambitions. But first, one last change was required in the nature of the ruling elite.

2 | Dictatorship and war

During the 1970s, the Ba'athist leadership witnessed a subtle change toward greater centralization of power. The Ba'ath Party was never a great example of a democratic institution with a strict practice of top-down appointments and limits on freedom of expression. Yet within the leading elite, which did include a few elements from outside the Sunni Tikriti core, a notion of collective leadership did exist. By the end of the decade, the conspiratorial atmosphere that dominated the party allowed the numerous overlapping intelligence services to rise to prominence. They came to control not only all aspects of society but also of the army and the party itself. Within these security groups, ideology came a distant second to personal allegiance and a strict code of discipline. In many ways, the rise of Saddam Hussein's dictatorship can be understood in terms of the ascendancy of the secret police over the party and the army. Recruits to these apparatuses came overwhelmingly from the rural tribal areas close to Saddam's own tribe, the Al Bu Nasir. In 1979, Ahmad Hasan al-Bakr, the veteran Ba'athist officer and President of Iraq since 1968, resigned supposedly for health reasons in favor of Saddam Hussein. Saddam assumed the presidency at a particularly challenging time for Iraq. A year had passed since Egypt, hitherto the undisputed leader of the Arab world, suffered isolation for its peace treaty with Israel and Iraq was eager to fill the vacuum. Then, scarcely a year later, Iran erupted into a popular revolution which shook the entire Middle East. Lest anyone have any doubt about his determination and ruthlessness, Saddam's presidency was inaugurated with a terrifying televised show trial of leading Ba'athist cadres, twenty-one of whom were later executed. As he coldly watched the spectacle of the trial, Saddam dismissed their pleas for mercy by saying: "It is not my fault if they were the slopes who sought equality with the peak."[1] As unsavory as he was, Saddam's hold on power proved extremely effective and he would go on to survive numerous wars, uprisings and coups to rule longer than any other leader of modern Iraq.

The regime's social base

On the social level, the rise of Saddam Hussein was the result of a social transformation that was several decades in the making. The destruction of the old landed elite after the 1958 Revolution, followed by the ascendancy of elements from Sunni rural backgrounds, set the stage for a more sectarian and ultimately tribal hierarchy. At this point, though, the regime was still not committed to a purely sectarian policy, and indeed it never officially adopted one. For example, the old urban Sunni classes which had dominated Iraqi politics under the monarchy were pushed to the background and some room was made available for Kurds and Shi'is to advance, provided they demonstrated strong loyalty to the regime. Networks created by state largesse and patronage came to define the material foundation of the regime's social base. Sami Zubaida refers to this phenomenon as "Crony Capitalism": "Opportunities, loans, licenses and contracts were distributed in accordance with a logic of allegiance, kinship and patronage, with the regime clans and regions benefiting greatly. At the same time, the powerful men of the regime were free to expropriate any land or business they found desirable."[2]

A type of "primitive accumulation" through expropriation and redistribution created new entrepreneurial and landowning classes directly dependent on the regime. This first started under the Ba'ath in 1970/71 when around 60,000–70,000 Failis (Shi'i Kurds) were unceremoniously expelled and their properties expropriated. Then again in 1980/81, around 200,000 Shi'is were declared aliens and deported to Iran. According to a regime spokesman at the time, the "deportation procedures apply to any Iranian family whose loyalty to the homeland and revolution is not proven even if it has Iraqi nationality."[3] Many of these were prominent men whose businesses were distributed to the regime's supporters. This was the second time in Iraqi history that such a radical transformation had affected the nature of the country's bourgeoisie. The first took place during the 1940s when Baghdad's large and prosperous Jewish community was expelled. Taking their place as the country's largest commercial class were the urban Shi'is, who were then also eliminated by the Ba'ath largely in favor of Sunnis of rural background. While groups such as the Jubur and Dulaymi tribesmen dominated the security and military establishments, the Kubaysis tended to take the place of the Shi'i bourgeoisie. This they achieved through their contacts and through their role as contractors and middlemen for the government's many lucrative projects.

The leadership cult

Saddam's dictatorship was accompanied by a campaign of glorification unprecedented in the history of the modern Middle East. In the 1982 report of the Ba'ath's 9th Congress, Saddam takes a position above other leaders of the party. The report mentions him as "a leader of special type who emerged and developed in unique circumstances."[4] Michel Aflaq, the aging Syrian founder of the party, described the "Historic Leader" in almost mystical words: "In the crucial periods, through suffering and painful lessons of experience, something resembling a call ascends from the conscience of the nation to indicate things which are missed, to which those eligible among its sons respond and thus their life follows a clear path."[5]

The media presented him as the leader and protector of the Arabs and often of Muslims as a whole. Imposing statues of the "Necessary Leader"[6] stood in every square, giant murals showed his many accomplishments and security men periodically checked to make sure that his portrait hung in every house. His birthday was celebrated as a national holiday, daily television broadcasts showed him visiting "ordinary" people, swimming in the Tigris, taking a walk with his family or ranting endlessly before a nervous audience about anything from proper childcare to table manners. Several referendums on his presidency were held which naturally yielded a "yes" vote of over 99 percent.[7] Streets, public squares, canals, and entire cities bore his name. The media portrayed him as the embodiment of manhood and courage. In one of his speeches before a Ba'athist youth group Saddam was quoted as saying: "Once when I was very young, around 13 or 14, I could not sleep for three successive summers because [of] the bullet belts around my body as well as the revolver and the rifle I carried in my hands so that when the call came I would be ready. I want the enemy to lose hope when they catch sight of us."[8]

There were Saddam T-shirts, Saddam wristwatches, and Saddam thermometers. Editors of newspapers apparently saw nothing comical (or nauseating) about reporting such events as Saddam granting the Saddam Prize for photography to Saddam's private photographer in a ceremony held at the Saddam Center for the Arts. Students were instructed to say "May God Protect Him" after mentioning his name. This had a particularly strong connotation in Iraq since Muslims are instructed to say such phrases as "Peace Be Upon Him" after the Prophet Muhammad's name. More to the point, some "historian" suddenly discovered that Saddam's family tree linked him directly to the Prophet's family. He even had, in the manner of the old caliphs, a regular court poet, 'Abdul-Razzaq 'Abdul-Wahid, who was handsomely rewarded for such lines as: "Your light shines bright, you who have given all your being to God." No goal was too lofty for the "Leader-Knight." Though he was a civilian and had been rejected for admission to military school, he was made Staff Field Marshal in 1979. A film about Saddam entitled *The Long Days*, which all schoolchildren and government employees had to watch, portrayed him as an infallible hero dedicated to serving his people. The actor who played the young Saddam was forbidden to appear in any other role. Several years later this same actor was branded a traitor and shot.

The Islamist challenge

From day one, Khomeini's Islamic Revolution in Iran was seen as a threat to the stability of the region as a whole. Like most revolutionary leaders, Iran's new rulers were quite optimistic about exporting their revolution. Iraq, with its majority Shi'i population and a growing religious opposition, was a prime target as Khomeini repeatedly urged Iraqis to overthrow the "atheist" Ba'athist regime. In one broadcast addressing the people of Iraq he said: "Wake up and topple this corrupt regime in your Islamic country before it is too late."[9] A report of the Ba'ath Party, written in 1982, expressed concern that revolutionary contagion was affecting its own rank and file: "The spread of fake religious practices among some Party members down to the level of Junior Supporters had created a state of relative entanglement between the base of the Party and those of religious-political parties [...] This had contributed to weakening the Party's alertness towards the growth of the hostile religious-political phenomenon."[10]

The spread of Islamist political parties in Iraq was part of a much broader phenomenon which affected the entire Middle East at the end of the 1970s. Their basic arguments were not so different from the nationalist and socialist ideas of the 1950s which focused on development and social justice. Like the nationalists, the Islamists sought to reverse the decay of society, restore a lost greatness, and guard against Western hegemony. Islamists tended to emphasize the problem of moral decay and laid a rather dubious claim to being more "authentic" than other movements which owed their ideas to foreign sources. In this respect, a common slogan of the Islamists was "Neither East nor West, but an Islamic Government." They argued that only through the establishment of an Islamic government with the authority to impose Islamic law can prosperity, justice, and independence be achieved. In Iraq, branches of the Egyptian-based Sunni Muslim Brothers Party developed in the 1950s, though its influence remained limited. The greatest religious opposition to the state came from the Shi'i community. Shi'ism in Iraq is as old as the schism which divided Islam in the mid-seventh century. Initially representing an argument over the nature of leadership after the death of Prophet Muhammad, the division soon encompassed other theological matters. Shi'ism remained mostly an oppressed sect, though at times it did contribute important figures and even established some principalities in Iraq. As an oppressed group it was instinctively suspicious of the state, developed strong traditions of autonomy, and a hierarchical religious establishment largely absent in Sunni Islam. By the end of Ottoman rule, the leading men of religion gained the title of Marja' al-Taqlid, or "Source of Emulation," and not long afterward a single paramount Marja' al-Taqlid emerged. Such a hierarchy did not preclude the development of intense, often violent, struggles between competing clerical families where even the paramount Marja' was simply considered a sort of first among equals. In addition to coping under Sunni rule, the other factor that influenced the nature of Iraqi Shi'ism was the mass conversion of numerous tribes arriving from Arabia during the eighteenth century. Because of their recent conversion, Arab tribal customs tended to dominate their notions of religious interpretation. This stood in stark contrast to the more urbane, Persian culture of the religious establishment in Iran. Such divisions, including class tensions, urban–rural and regional differences, constantly disrupted the formation of a single Shi'i political movement.

With the establishment of modern Iraq after the First World War, Shi'i activism focused on demands for greater inclusion, rather than the separatist ideas common among the Kurds. Gains were made throughout the monarchic period but hopes for equality were especially boosted after the 1958 Revolution. Under the Ba'ath, however, they rarely achieved prominent positions though they did make up the majority of the rank and file membership. Repression under the Ba'ath, including the previously-mentioned mass expulsions, drove young Shi'is toward the opposition, especially the Communist Party. The most important of the opposition religious parties in the 1980s was the Islamic Da'wa Party. Influenced by the Muslim Brothers, Shi'i leaders such as the senior cleric Muhammad Baqir al-Sadr helped found the party in 1957. Other than pushing for greater equality, their main concern at that time was losing control over religious schools, courts, and welfare institutions to the secular state. Mostly, however, they feared the growing influence of the Communist Party over young Shi'is. The Da'wa Party represented something quite new in Shi'i circles in that its members demonstrated an allegiance to an ideology and organization rather than to an individual cleric or family. Also, its members were tied together through modern party mechanisms rather than networks of patronage. In emphasizing this point to their rank and file, the Da'wa's official organ wrote:

> The party is based on the principle of *shura* [consultation], and it is based on the idea of difference of points of views. [...] This means voting is the base for the leadership structure of the party, the party's Congress system and local *shura* in any area. [...] The will of the Congress of the party is superior to that of the Leadership.[11]

Despite al-Sadr's moral guidance, the Da'wa's leaders were mainly laymen of urban middle-class backgrounds. After the fall of the monarchy, it participated, with very modest results, in student and labor union elections. With the rise of the Ba'ath they faced increasing repression which intensified greatly after the Iranian Revolution of 1979. Al-Sadr and his sister were executed and hundreds of activists were rounded up during the ensuing demonstrations. Other groups included followers of the Hakim family, who later formed the Supreme Council of the Islamic Revolution in Iraq (SCIRI), and followers of the fiery young cleric, Muhammad Sadiq al-Sadr (sometimes called Sadr II). Yet these were organizations based on traditional personal loyalty and suffered from the weaknesses of such informal groups.

Saddam's eight-year war

The view from Saddam's palace of the Iranian Revolution was two-fold. First, it was seen as a danger, especially after the Da'wa, with assistance from Tehran, carried out a number of assassinations of top Ba'athists, and held several anti-regime demonstrations. Second, the post-revolutionary chaos in Iran, the break-up of the armed forces, and the international isolation it suffered after the taking of US hostages, was seen as a golden opportunity to deal with a historic enemy and achieve the status of sole regional power in the oil-rich Gulf. Going back to Ottoman times, the border with Iran, especially in the south, was always in dispute. In 1975, Saddam himself had to sign a humiliating treaty with the late Shah, bowing to Iranian territorial demands in return for an end to Iranian assistance to the Kurdish rebels. In addition to regaining lost territories, Saddam sought to secure Iraq's southern outlet to the sea for oil exports and perhaps even to lay claim to parts of oil-rich southwestern Iran. But fear of Iranian "conspiracies" to overthrow the regime far outweighed all other considerations; fears shared equally by the conservative Arab monarchs of the Gulf. In 1980, Saddam gave logistical and material support to a number of dissident Iranian army officers to carry out a coup against the Khomeini regime. The "Nozeh coup," as it was known, ended in spectacular failure and served only to sour relations further. Shortly thereafter, Saddam abrogated the 1975 treaty and ordered the army's commanders to prepare for war.

In September 1980, Iraqi tanks rolled across the border at several points simultaneously. At first Iraqi troops met with such timid resistance that most observers felt the war would last only a couple of months at the most. Both the United States and the Soviet Union, alarmed at Iranian radicalism, remained neutral during the early phase of the war. Within the Arab world divisions appeared more clearly than ever before, with Iraq receiving strong support (financial and military) from the Arab Gulf countries, Jordan and Egypt. Yet, even here, the support was not free from contradictions. The Gulf countries were willing to do what they could to resist Iranian advances but they did not wish to see Saddam's missiles hanging over their heads either. With this in mind, Iraq was refused membership in the newly established Gulf Cooperation Council. Jordan put its port facilities at the disposal of Iraq, making a hefty profit along the way. Egypt provided military assistance, but also insisted on having up to one million of its migrant laborers work in Iraq earning scarce foreign currency. Syria and Libya, on the other hand, unambiguously supported Iran. Syria, in particular, dealt Iraq a painful blow by shutting the Iraqi oil pipelines which run across its territory to the Mediterranean. After a couple of months Iranian resistance seemed to grow more stubborn as internal differences were set aside to combat the invasion. As the war dragged on, Iranian forces began to switch from defensive to offensive operations and in 1982 a large Iranian offensive drove the Iraqis back across the border with heavy loses. This defeat nearly brought Saddam down as several army officers, top Ba'athist officials, and even some members of his family, held him responsible for the setbacks. Yet, Iranian announcements of their intention to carry on to Baghdad itself caused the Iraqi military command to close ranks around the regime.

Another consequence of the Iraqi setback was the shift in American policy from neutrality to active support for Iraq. To the Americans, the prospect of Iranian Revolutionary Guards marching all the way to Baghdad, threatening Kuwait and Saudi Arabia, and thereby controlling the oil of this strategic region, was a scenario of nightmarish proportions. The ideal outcome, from this perspective, was for both sides to grow weaker with neither achieving a clear victory. To establish a balance, the Americans gave the Iraqis sophisticated intelligence on Iranian troop movements utilizing satellites and AWAC planes, and facilitated Iraqi access to military technology. US corporations, such as Hewlett-Packard and Bechtel, were encouraged to sell equipment which was later used in the making of chemical and biological weapons, and in the development of the nuclear program. Throughout the war, the United States turned a blind eye to Iraq's increasing use of internationally banned chemical weapons. Iraq also received agricultural imports on favorable terms and important diplomatic support. This encouraged other powers, notably France, Germany, and the Soviet Union, to act in a similar fashion. Much of this assistance was arranged during a secret meeting between special envoy Donald Rumsfeld and Saddam held in 1983.

By 1984, the war had bogged down into a form of trench warfare. Iranian leaders had hoped that at least part of the Iraqi army, composed overwhelmingly of Shi'i soldiers, would rebel against Sunni rule. The Iraqi army, however, held together even during the worst of the fighting mainly because Iraqi Shi'is have a deep sense of their Arab identity and never demonstrated a desire for unity with Iran. Unlike the Kurds, their struggle has been mostly defined by demands for greater inclusion within the state, rather than separation or autonomy. At various stages of the war, a number of Shi'i tribes organized independent resistance to Iranian incursions in spite of their historic animosity to Saddam's regime. To an extent, the unity of the Iraqi army, even when the country appeared to be on the brink of military collapse, is testimony to the strength of Iraqi nationalism by this time. As one veteran of the war who hails from a leading Shi'i clerical family once told me: "I never thought of defecting because I am Iraqi not Iranian."[12] Nevertheless, Ba'athist terror and collective punishment also played a role as soldiers knew only too well what would become of their families back home should they consider rebellion.

The Iraqis had the advantage of superior organization and equipment, while the Iranians' main asset was the revolutionary zeal of their troops and a complete disregard for casualties. William Polk, who visited the Iraq front in 1983, made the following observations:

What I saw were surely the most bizarre battlefields in the history of warfare. [...] Miles of trenched tank traps knifed through the desert guaranteeing protection against the nonexistent Persian armor; row after neat row of late-model Russian armored personnel carriers and partially dug-in tanks were protected by batteries of surface to-air-missiles. I was supposed to be impressed and I was. But what really struck me was that even the dugout of the captain commanding a company on the front-line was air-conditioned and illuminated by television.[13]

This contrasts sharply with a reporter's description of the Iranian side:

The Iranian front lines tend to be scenes of chaos and dedication, with turbaned mullahs, rifles slung on their backs, rushing about on brightly colored motorcycles encouraging the troops. Religious slogans are posted everywhere, and sometimes reinforcements arrive cheerfully carrying their own coffins as a sign of their willingness to be "martyred."[14]

Despite the Iraqi advantage, Iran kept up the pressure with its terrible "human waves" tactics resulting in especially high casualties. In 1986, with an eye on the major city of Basra, they managed another breakthrough in the south by seizing control of the Faw peninsula, cutting off Iraq's only access to the sea. It was at this point that the Americans stepped up their assistance even further and began to engage the Iranians directly in the Gulf. The result was the virtual destruction of the small Iranian navy and a limited obstruction of Iranian oil exports. Encouraged by this new American commitment, Iraq launched a series of attacks, including a particularly bloody battle to take back Faw in which mustard gas was used extensively, resulting in a complete rout for the Iranians. Even more terrible was the Iraqi attack on the Kurdish town of Halabja (population around 50,000) in 1988. Throughout the war, the Kurdish opposition parties had supported Iran. Partly out of revenge, and partly because there was reason to believe that Kurdish forces had taken the town, Halabja was subjected to sustained aerial bombardment using chemical weapons resulting in the immediate death of around 5,000 of its inhabitants. Estimates vary but some point to as many as 12,000 dying later after suffering untold pains. As news filtered out, reporters were eventually permitted to visit the town from the Iranian side a few days later. Here's one description:

> Dead bodies – human and animal – littered the streets, huddled in doorways, slumped over the steering wheels of their cars. Survivors stumbled around, laughing hysterically, before collapsing [...] Those who had been directly exposed to the gas found that their symptoms worsened as the night wore on. Many children died along the way and were abandoned where they fell.[15]

Such descriptions and several gruesome pictures showing parents cradling their children in a last vain attempt to flee, helped to create an international outcry. Nevertheless, neither the United States nor the Soviet Union took any meaningful measures to address Iraq's use of these outlawed weapons. Facing the prospect of a direct war with the United States with a completely ruined economy, Iran finally chose to put an end to the eight-year conflict. For Khomeini, who had pushed his countrymen on despite heavy losses, this was, in his words, a decision "more deadly than poison."

The cost of war

The war with Iran triggered Iraq's economic free-fall. Prior to the war, Iraq had a healthy reserves of around $35 billion. By the time the ceasefire was declared, it was indebted to the tune of $110 billion, half of which was owed to the Arab Gulf countries. With around a million men in arms, out of a total population of around 22 million, the war was eating up about $20 billion per year. Some economists have estimated that the war cost Iraq about 87 percent of its GNP. Flush with huge oil earnings and foolishly expecting a short campaign, Saddam tried to insulate the general population by proceeding to spend lavishly on both military and non-military imports during the first two years of the war. Thus, from 1978 to 1981, imports soared from $4.2 billion to $20.5 billion, an increase of nearly 500 percent. Contracts on non-military projects signed with foreign firms climbed from $14.8 billion in 1980 to $24.3 billion the following year. This "Guns and Butter" policy ground to a halt as the war dragged on and as Iranian shelling managed to close down

Iraq's oil exports from the south. Syria also assisted Iran by closing the Iraqi pipeline running across its territories.[16] As a result, the income from oil plummeted from a high of $23.3 billion in 1980 to $7.8 billion in 1983. Table 2.1 demonstrates how non-productive military imports came to dominate Iraqi trade so that, by 1984, arms accounted for a massive 93 percent of all imports, and continued to be high even after the end of the war.

In 1982, Iraq announced the first steps of austerity measures to counter its economic plight. As the Gross Domestic Product fell, so too did economic growth. In order to maintain the high level of spending needed to prosecute the war, the state resorted to de-investment and to heavy borrowing especially from Kuwait, Saudi Arabia, and the United Arab Emirates, all of which would figure prominently in Saddam's second war. Assistance was also received, as noted above, from the United States, the Soviet Union, and France. In return, Saddam handed out generous contracts to Western and Soviet firms and adjusted the border in favor of Saudi Arabia and Kuwait. He also reached agreement with Turkey, allowing it to enter Iraqi territory to attack Kurdish guerrillas in return for an expansion of Iraq's northern oil pipeline which goes through Turkish territory. Such agreements and concessions still could not stem the tide of

TABLE 2.1 Trade and arms imports, 1980–89 ($ billion)

Year	Exports	Imports	Arms imports	Ratio of arms to total imports
1980	26.3	13.8	2.4	17.4
1981	10.6	20.5	4.2	20.5
1982	10.3	21.5	7.1	33.0
1983	9.4	10.3	7.0	68.0
1984	9.4	9.9	9.2	93.0
1985	10.7	10.5	4.7	44.8
1986	7.6	8.7	5.7	65.5
1987	11.4	7.4	5.5	74.3
1988	11.0	10.6	4.6	45.0
1989	14.5	13.8	2.7	19.6

Source: A. Alnasrawi, "Economic Devastation, Underdevelopment and Outlook," in Hazelton (ed.), *Iraq Since the Gulf War*, p. 88.

economic decline most noticeable in the high inflation rates and the devaluation of the Iraqi currency from a rate of 1:0.3 to the dollar to 1:5. By the mid-1980s, Iraq would fall behind all other countries in the region in such sectors as health, education, average incomes, and investment. In terms of life expectancy and infant mortality, Iraq fell behind even such non-oil-producing countries as Syria and Jordan. Food per capita production fell by 30 percent of what it had been prior to the war, causing the country to depend even more on imports and fueling inflation. As might be expected, priority in domestic production was given to the arms industry. By 1987 the military accounted for 30.2 percent of GNP as opposed to 4.6 percent for education and 0.8 percent for health. Such spending continued even after the war, despite the pressing need to repair the massive damage done to the oil industry. Saddam also sought to reduce the possibility of rebellion by favoring the all-important capital of Baghdad over other regions when considering economic development.

The war affected the regime's social policies in more than one way. We have already noted the rise in anti-Persian propaganda and legislation, including the deportation decisions. Other laws were passed to reinforce a racist bent. History books were rewritten to demonstrate the presence of an Arab–Persian conflict since time immemorial. The Arab element was always pure and chivalrous, while the Persian was always evil and traitorous. Even Islam was presented as having a true Arab "essence" with Iran constantly trying to corrupt it through heretical notions. Men who had married Iranian women were rewarded with handsome government grants if they divorced their wives. Women were simply prohibited from marrying non-Arab men. True to its practice of collective punishment, the regime declared that the wives and children of deserters would be held accountable and arrested. Saddam, constantly worried by the Iranian advantage in population, took measures aimed at increasing the birthrate in Iraq by outlawing contraceptives and abortion, both of which had been legal for decades. An additional step was made through his declaration that every mother should have at least five children. Politically, the regime took several measures to ensure its survival. While Shi'is continued to comprise the majority of the rank and file of the Ba'ath Party and even of its general security services, the special forces charged with protecting the president and his family were increasingly drawn from the Sunni Arab tribal areas. The sense of hostility and alienation of these recruits to the urban population intensified the aura of fear and terror which accompanied any dealings with the regime. Isam al-Khafaji, who interviewed a member of the special forces in the early 1990s, wrote of the mentality and sense of devotion that these officials had:

> The Jubur tribe has been one of the main pools for the recruitment of the intelligence personnel, including the *Jihaz* [the special forces]. A Juburi NCO in the *Jihaz* told me how he, like many of his fellow tribesmen, had spent his childhood in al-Sharqat[17] dreaming of Baghdad. He recalled his first visit there in 1987, how he felt when he saw a shower for the first time and the thrill of touching the "soft flesh" of women in the Baghdad Sheraton. No brain-washing was needed to turn envy of the lavish lifestyle of "soft" city dwellers, especially Baghdadis, into a sense of gratitude and devotion towards those who enabled the *Jihaz* recruits to conquer that alien city. And conquer it they did.[18]

Aside from all this, there was a profound sense of futility about the whole disastrous episode. Perhaps never in the entire history of mankind have so many died and suffered only to return to the pre-war status quo. The Iran–Iraq War was the longest, most destructive conflict since the Second World War. During the eight years of relentless slaughter, a whole generation reached adulthood not knowing the meaning of peace and most of the men experienced the horrors of the battlefield first-hand. This had a massive psychological impact on the population. No one knows the exact figures but the number of dead on both sides could very well exceed 1.3 million, with Iraq suffering anywhere from 250,000 to 500,000 losses. In the battle to retake Faw, Iraq alone lost around 50,000 soldiers. Such abstract numbers, however, fail to capture the sheer brutality that Iranian and Iraqi men had to acclimatize themselves to. One veteran of the war spoke to me of the "animal rage" he felt toward Iranian soldiers facing him across the front lines. He added: "At those moments, if I had the chance, I would have thought nothing of killing them, their wives and children. It was irrational anger."[19] According to one Iranian eyewitness: "I have seen young boys burned alive. I have seen Iranian and Iraqi boys tearing each other literally with their nails and teeth. It is raging hate against raging hate."[20]

Even those who were spared the horrors of the battlefields were not immune from its impact. Scarcely a family was free from the trauma of losing a close member and men with missing limbs or some other permanent malady were apparent everywhere. The high death rate among men led to a perceptible increase in the number of widows and unmarried women. In a society which places a premium on marriage and parenthood, this, in turn, led to various moral and ethical problems. Families were also traumatized by the large numbers of soldiers missing in action or rumored to have been captured. This writer is personally acquainted with several cases where soldiers would return only to find that their wives had remarried, a horrific taboo in Islamic culture. An entire generation grew disturbingly accustomed to dealing with death, suffering and the breakdown of ethical values. A reporter who arrived shortly after one particularly savage battle described this "indifference to death":

> "We crushed the Iranians like insects," said an Iraqi soldier, jubilation showing through the exhaustion on his face. He squatted in a frontline trench he was sharing with three dusty Iranian corpses which, after two days, remained unburied. In the hot sun, the Iraqis' own dead still lay in the open where they had fallen, their limbs convulsed in death agonies. [...] This indifference to death [...] was hard to believe.[21]

Beyond this suffering there was also a sense of resentment against those who did not experience the war, a resentment which created a new fissure in Iraqi society. But it also spilled out beyond Iraq's borders. Many in Iraq felt that they had suffered only to protect an ungrateful Arab world from Iranian expansion. In 1990, after Saddam had put Iraq on course for another, even more destructive war, one student voiced what was surely a common feeling in the aftermath of the Iran war: "The Kuwaitis boast of their aid to Iraq, but it was Iraq that defended their thrones and wealth with blood. We sacrificed our brothers, fathers and sons to let them enjoy life."[22]

With the dictatorship becoming even more oppressive and still armed to the teeth, an economy on the brink of collapse, and a society heavily scarred and accustomed to a culture of violence, it was not too difficult to see the seeds of a new conflict brewing.

3 | Imperialism and the crisis of Kuwait

The end of the war with Iran was received with an outpouring of joy throughout Iraq lasting several days. This, however, was short-lived as Iraqis soon became aware of a new war which had already started, even before the signing of the ceasefire with Iran. Saddam was intent upon settling scores with his internal enemies even if they included entire communities. The Kurds were especially apprehensive about what the ceasefire might mean for them. Kurdish nationalists had actively supported Iran and taken advantage of the army's preoccupation at the front to extend their control over vast areas of the north. Tensions were likewise brewing in Baghdad itself, where the regime's promises of the peace and prosperity awaiting Iraqis after the war were met with the reality of scarcity and continuing state terror. The end of the Iran war also coincided with the collapse of the Soviet Union and the socialist bloc. While this brought an end to the political dynamics defined by the Cold War, it specifically affected Iraq in two ways. First, it represented a blow to the "development ethos" which had been the backbone of Ba'athist economic thinking since the mid-1960s. Second, it encouraged the US to take a more aggressive posture in the region.

Saddam's "Final Solution"

Even before the end of the war, the regime was contemplating a comprehensive program to resolve the "Kurdish problem" once and for all. In addition to Iraq, Kurdish-speaking peoples, currently numbering some 25 million, are also present in southeastern Turkey, northwestern Iran and a corner of northeastern Syria. The Kurds are a linguistically, ethnically, and culturally distinct nationality and form around 20 percent of the population in Iraq. At the same time, centuries of interaction have created strong religious and economic bonds between Iraqi Kurdish cities such as Sulaymaniya,

Irbil, Kirkuk, and others, with Arab Iraq. Of the 5 to 6 million Kurds in Iraq, as many as 2 million live in the Arab cities of Mosul and Baghdad. Since the end of the First World War, a number of Kurdish national leaders have emerged to lobby and at times fight for an independent homeland. Iraq had the best organized Kurdish nationalist movement which periodically raised rebellions during various periods of modern Iraqi history. The most famous Iraqi Kurdish personality was the indefatigable Mullah Mustafa al-Barzani whose Kurdish Democratic Party suffered a blow in 1975 only to re-emerge under his son's leadership during the Iran–Iraq War. The other important Kurdish organization was the Patriotic Union of Kurdistan led by Jalal Talbani about whom more will be said later. With Iranian support, Kurdish nationalists succeeded in establishing full control over large areas of the countryside and some towns. They also regularly harassed the Iraqi army and, at times, directly coordinated their attacks with Iranian offensives.

Beginning in 1987, when Saddam, with US assistance, felt strong enough, the regime initiated an eight-part campaign aimed at the complete depopulation of large areas of the Kurdish north and the final destruction of the Kurdish national movement. The campaign, code-named "Anfal" in reference to a chapter in the Qur'an dealing with the spoils of war, gradually expanded to the point where organizations such as Human Rights Watch later labeled it a genocide. Much is known about the details of this campaign since many documents and recordings dealing with it later fell into Kurdish and US hands. A cousin of Saddam, Ali Hasan al-Majid, nicknamed "Chemical Ali" by the Kurds, who was particularly prone to savagery, oversaw the campaign. In one recording of May 1988, he can be heard speaking to a group of Ba'athist officials: "I will kill them all with chemical weapons! Who is going to say anything? The international community? Fuck them! The international community, and those who listen to them."[1] In fact, a variety of chemical weapons was used in a flurry of indiscriminate bombings of villages. Helicopters were ordered to fly low and kill every living thing, including livestock, to make sure that the area would remain uninhabited. Where possible, the campaign specifically targeted all men aged fifteen to fifty, who were rounded up and shot. Human Rights Watch, basing itself on several eyewitness testimonies, described scenes reminiscent of the Nazi holocaust:

> Some groups of prisoners were lined up, shot from the front, and dragged into pre-dug mass graves; others were made to lie down in pairs, sardine-style, next to mounds of fresh corpses, before being killed; still others were tied together, made to stand on the lip of the pit, and shot in the back so that they would fall forward into it – a method that was presumably more efficient from the point of view of the killers. Bulldozers then pushed earth or sand loosely over the heaps of corpses. Some of the grave sites contained dozens of separate pits and obviously contained the bodies of thousands of victims.[2]

Over 100,000 refugees poured into Turkey with tens of thousands more going to Iran in an effort to escape the slaughter. Bulldozers usually moved in to ensure that the refugees would not return. The numbers are again only estimates but they range in the order of 180,000 killed (around 1 percent of the population), the destruction of 4,000 villages (90 percent of all villages) and twenty middle-sized towns. Hundreds of thousands, mainly the surviving women and children, were forcibly relocated to concentration camps from which many did not return. At one such camp near Kirkuk, survivors described the way they were processed:

> Men and women were segregated on the spot as soon as the trucks had rolled to a halt in the base's large central courtyard or parade ground. The process was brutal [...] A little later, the men were further divided by age, small children were kept with their mothers, and the elderly and infirm were shunted off to separate quarters. Men and teenage boys considered to be of an age to use a weapon were herded together. Roughly speaking, this meant males of between fifteen and fifty, but there was no rigorous check of identity documents, and strict chronological age seems to have been less of a criterion than size and appearance.[3]

As many as 15 million landmines were then planted around the sites and all across the border areas. The plight of refugees drew international condemnation but little else was done. The success of the Anfal campaign encouraged Saddam to launch similar attacks against Shi'i rebels hiding in the southern marsh areas. The intensity of these attacks did not reach the same level, but plans were drawn up for the draining of the marsh areas, resulting in a human as well as an ecological catastrophe.

The question of weapons of mass destruction

Saddam's liberal use of chemical weapons alarmed a number of Middle Eastern countries and eventually contributed to the souring of relations with the US. As far back as 1972, only a few years after the Ba'ath seizure of power, the regime secretly established a program for the development of nuclear, chemical, and biological weapons. Iraqi leaders were always worried about Iranian intentions, especially given its overwhelming advantage in population. Ba'athist leaders, among whom was Saddam, became especially concerned after 1971 when Iran forcibly seized three contested islands near the mouth of the Persian Gulf. Knowing that they faced a militarily superior foe, the Ba'athist leadership opted for such a program to form a "strategic equalizer" to Iranian ambitions. They also felt that an arsenal of such weapons of mass destruction (WMD) would help position Iraq as a leader of the Arab world in its conflict with Israel. The program proceeded slowly, facing serious technical and political setbacks. The most serious setback occurred in 1981 when the Israeli air force destroyed the Osirak nuclear reactor. By the middle of the war with Iran, Iraq was able to deploy chemical weapons, and while it never publicly acknowledged their use, privately it justified its actions as being necessary to halt the Iranian advance. As noted in the previous chapter, this was apparently accepted by the West, the socialist bloc, and many Arab countries as they all turned a blind eye to Iraqi acquisition of the products needed for its WMD program. A later Congressional inquiry into the matter accused the Reagan administration of "secretly court[ing] Saddam Hussein with reckless abandon."[4] One company in Maryland that sold Iraq stock for anthrax and botulism was investigated but later given Commerce Department approval.

After the end of the war, Saddam renewed the emphasis on developing a domestic military industry with the WMD program as its centerpiece. This was yet another indication that Saddam tended to lack faith in a program of patient, long-term economic develop-ment as the path toward postwar reconstruction, favoring instead the language of confrontation and war. Later inspections would reveal that Iraq had the capability to produce its own medium-range missiles and warheads. It had also manufactured large amounts of anthrax and botulinum toxin. Anthrax was especially dangerous since only one gram had the potential to kill 100 million people. Chemical weapons included VX, Sarin, Tabun, and mustard gas, and the nuclear program was not far from producing a crude atomic weapon. Desperate for economic assistance and eager to shore up his position in the Arab world, Saddam began to warn of his willingness to use WMD to protect Iraq's "rights." Initially, the target of such threats was Israel, where the state media suddenly focused on the Jewish state's known possession of nuclear weapons. In one speech given in 1989 prior to his invasion of Kuwait, Saddam vowed that "if Israel attacks any Arab country [including Iraq's nuclear reactors ...] we have the means to burn half of Israel." Such saber-rattling natu-rally raised alarm in Israel and the US.

Economic liberalization

While threats and destructive weapons were one way of address-ing the need for economic assistance, some of Saddam's advisers convinced him of the need to restructure the Iraqi economy altogether. The operative word here was "*infitah*" or "openness." Essentially meaning the general economic liberalization and privat-ization of industries, *infitah* was not new to the Middle East. It had started with much fanfare in Egypt in 1973, in an effort to deal with the inefficiencies of state-run enterprises and bloated bureaucracies. Prior to the war, Iraq was able to mask the growing inefficiencies of its economy with lucrative oil exports. The drop in the volume of oil exports due to Iranian closure of Iraq's southern ports, and the fall in oil prices from a high of $35 per barrel in 1980 to as low as $15 in 1988, made this more difficult. The Iraqi economy, like that of most oil exporters, had become structurally accustomed to high oil revenues and the sharp drop in prices forced many countries to seek ways of cutting state spending and off-loading productive activities to the private sector. Likewise, the reduction in oil revenues, along with the massive spending on military imports, created a chronic shortage of foreign currency, which in turn put more pressure on the economy. The decline of the Soviet Union and the socialist bloc also had an impact since they reduced their technical and trade supports which had benefited Iraq since the early 1970s. It likewise called into question the whole "development ethos" which had been championed by the socialist bloc and applied in many Third World countries. Throughout the world the emphasis was now shifting from social objectives to market reforms as capitalism seemed to emerge triumphant.

With the end of the war came the added problem of demobilization of the massive one-million-man army. The state had to find an alternative to past guarantees of jobs and welfare services. In 1987, and especially 1988, Saddam approved a broad program of privatization that went well beyond Egypt's famed *infitah* of the early 1970s. Practically all factories producing consumer goods were sold, as were large sections of the service sector (hotels for example). Leasing of some state enterprises, such as petrol stations, was permitted, the investment ceiling was lifted, and a series of measures, such as the Arab Investment Law of 1989, were taken to encourage Arab investment. To entice the private sector further, a law was passed facilitating the importation of cheap labor from such Arab countries as Egypt and Yemen. Of major importance were the reforms affecting agriculture. Despite its huge potential, agriculture was in serious decline and the high price of food imports placed special urgency on the development of this sector. Laws were passed allowing the leasing of state farms, while the large state-owned poultry and dairy farms were sold outright. Land confiscated in previous land reforms or due to the regime's repeated deportations of whole communities, were distributed without delay.

Economically, the results were mixed. Agriculture showed a marked improvement with production doubling, yet industry tended to decline even further mainly due to the limited availability of spare parts and raw materials. In one example, cited by Kiren Chaudry, the privatized Dialah tomato-canning factory, which had previously imported fresh tomatoes from Czechoslovakia, was now forced to cut labor, use only domestic tomatoes, and hike prices by 43 percent to make ends meet.[5] Even more important, potential private investors, especially the coveted Arab bourgeoisie, were never really enticed into risking their capital in Iraq. The regime did not exactly have a good reputation when it came to honoring property rights, nor did its repressive state and heavy dependence on patronage encourage a climate of secure investments. Lastly, the regime, for all its apparent radical reforms, never relinquished its tight control over such essential matters as international communications and foreign currency exchange. Still, a limited section of the Iraqi bourgeoisie with strong ties to the regime's inner circle, such as the Buniya family, did manage to enrich itself. The only immediate changes for the rest of the population were a steep rise in unemployment (previously unheard of in Iraq), a brisk black market in currency exchange, soaring inflation of nearly 60 percent, severe shortages, and a growing gap between rich and poor.

Most of the burden fell on the salaried professional and working classes whose incomes were eroded by inflation and who now had to live with the devastating risk of unemployment with no social safety-net. In the two years after the Iran war, Iraq witnessed the prospect of hundreds of thousands of soldiers roaming the streets with nothing to show for their sacrifices except unemployment and a return to the prewar status quo. As with Egypt's earlier reforms, the reaction in Iraq was spontaneous rioting, strikes and the radical politicization of the only space left outside state control: the mosque. The regime's powerful repressive apparatus managed to keep the lid on, but even Saddam must have known that this could not last for ever. Still, if any more repressive measures were needed, he was quick to authorize them. New measures such as abolishing labor unions (never independent to begin with), amending labor laws to allow for the lengthening of the work day, and overturning Acts on the right to employment, were intended to send a message both to the malcontents and to prospective investors of the regime's determination to carry out the reforms.

Such tensions might have been absorbed through some bold political reforms. The regime, however, took only token measures which were never taken seriously. In 1989, Saddam announced the formation of a committee charged with writing the country's first permanent constitution since the fall of the monarchy. In 1925, the British-supported monarchy had produced the country's only permanent constitution. It provided for a strong king, tribal laws in the countryside, and it denied women the vote, but it did prove functional for a while. After the revolution of 1958, the country witnessed a series of temporary constitutions, all of which claimed "the nation" as their source of legitimacy without once holding an election. The 1958 temporary constitution was notable for its reference to Iraq being a country of two nationalities, Arabs and Kurds, but it also concentrated power in the office of the prime minister. The constitution of 1963 placed increasing emphasis on the Arab identity of the country and the 1968 document even included a phrase stating that the state would work toward achieving Arab unity. Saddam's proposed constitution was to be put to a national referendum which would have surely returned the mandatory 99 percent approval were it not for his invasion of Kuwait and the deferral of all such schemes. One notable reference, which might be considered a change in Ba'athist policy, was to the permissibility of opposition parties and greater political "openness." Yet, such parties were required to have supported Iraq's war effort, to recognize the "special leadership" of Saddam, and to adhere to "the principles of the Ba'athist Revolution." The preamble leaves no doubt as to the focus of power by mentioning Saddam by name as the "symbol" of the country, the "son of the nation" and its great leader. The Ba'ath Party is also mentioned as having provided the correct guide for the future of the country.

Iraq also took a number of diplomatic measures to help alleviate its postwar problems. Regionally, diplomats rarely wasted an opportunity to remind the Arabs, especially the Gulf Arabs, that Iraq fought to safeguard the "Eastern Gate" of the Arab world against Iranian expansionism, and that it expected to be rewarded with favorable economic agreements and political alliances. Iraq tended to favor the establishment of regional economic and military alliances such as the Arab Cooperation Council. Created mainly at the insistence of Iraq, it also included Egypt, Jordan, and Yemen. Having failed to join the Gulf Cooperation Council, Iraq signed a separate non-aggression treaty with Saudi Arabia, and entered into what were initially quite cordial negotiations with Kuwait over borders and outstanding loans. Late in 1989, Kuwait's Emir Jaber was well received in Baghdad and decorated with the country's highest award. There were, likewise, no signs of outright tensions with the US as agreements on food imports were renewed.

The question of Kuwait

Such cordial relations with Kuwait and the West were never on solid ground, especially after the end of the Iran war and the subsequent problems of reconstruction. Iraq's internal crisis was the primary factor behind the gradual escalation of regional tensions eventually leading to a new war. Still, the historic background to the highly problematic Iraqi–Kuwaiti relations played a role in determining the language and intensity of the ensuing conflict. During most of Ottoman rule, Kuwait was a tiny rather insignificant fishing village nominally under the suzerainty of the Governor of Basra. As with the rural tribes in Iraq proper, Kuwait's tribal leaders rarely demonstrated active subservience to Ottoman authorities, but this hardly troubled the Ottomans who were not particularly concerned with this desert region. In 1869, as part of his centralizing efforts, Midhat Pasha, the Governor of Baghdad, ordered the stationing of a permanent garrison in Kuwait and took steps to enforce its incorporation into the province of Basra. There is little doubt that Kuwait would have gradually been absorbed into the Ottoman administration of Iraq but for British intervention at the end of the nineteenth century. In 1899, Britain signed a treaty of protection with Sheikh Mubarak al-Sabah of Kuwait. Though the Ottomans never recognized it, this treaty later became the basis for Kuwaiti claims of independence. In 1913, as war appeared more likely in Europe, Britain agreed to withdraw from this treaty and recognize full Ottoman sovereignty over Kuwait, but the First World War and the Ottomans' fateful decision to side with Germany scuttled this deal. After the war, British administrators under the direction of Sir Percy Cox, the British High Commissioner in Baghdad, arranged a conference to settle outstanding border issues in Arabia and Iraq. The so-called 'Uqayr Conference of 1922 was attended by Sheikh 'Abdul-'Aziz ibn Sa'ud from Arabia, officials representing King Faisal of Iraq and a British officer representing Emir Mubarak al-Sabah of Kuwait. After a series of heated arguments which, at times, reportedly left the great warrior ibn Sa'ud in tears, Percy Cox simply brandished his red pencil and forced the present boundaries on the parties. Iraq, though still under a British Mandate, refused to recognize the settlement and continued to make repeated claims to Kuwait. Iraqi leaders argued that not only was there a historic and administrative tie between Kuwait and the Ottoman province of Basra, but, more importantly, the viability of the future state of Iraq would suffer without a safe outlet to the sea.

Prior to the discovery of oil in Kuwait, Iraqi demands were not universally rejected by the inhabitants of the tiny Emirate. Most of the merchant and landowning classes continued to have strong interests in Basra and many saw their inclusion into a wealthier and more powerful country as a source of security against the designs of the Saudis, who weren't exactly satisfied with Cox's red lines either. Prior to the 1930s, even the Emir of Kuwait himself held more property in Basra than in Kuwait. The British also had second thoughts. As late as 1930, Major Hubert Young, acting High Commissioner in Baghdad, recommended the gradual incorporation of Kuwait by Iraq for both economic and security reasons. Iraq repeated its claims after its independence in 1932, and again after the 1958 Revolution. By then, however, oil had been discovered and neither the Kuwaitis nor their British protectors were now willing to consider sharing it. In 1961, a major crisis developed after Britain declared its intention to withdraw from Kuwait and recognize its full independence. General Qasim declared Iraqi sovereignty over Kuwait and moved troops to the border. The British, however, sent additional reinforcements to prevent a sudden invasion. This was followed by a meeting of the Arab League which recognized Kuwaiti independence and authorized Egypt to send troops to protect it. Qasim grudgingly pulled Iraqi forces back but refused to back down politically. After Qasim's overthrow Iraq did recognize the independence of Kuwait but tensions remained over border disagreements. Under the Ba'ath, relations periodically soured over border disputes but during the Iran–Iraq War they mostly tended to be warm.

Toward a new war

Repression, diplomacy, and dubious promises of political reforms did little to defuse the mounting crisis born of eight years of war and sudden market reforms. The months leading up to Iraq's fateful invasion of its small Arab neighbor and one-time ally were full of twists and turns which are beyond the scope of this survey. Gregory Gause has argued convincingly that Saddam's decision to go to war was not simply the result of his predisposition for violence (though this is undeniable), but rather it was mainly due to his conviction that he faced a real foreign conspiracy aimed at overthrowing his regime. Saddam's grievances focused on two points: loans and oil. Ba'athist leaders were rather frank about the impasse they found themselves in. In a meeting of Ba'athist cadres after Iraq had already invaded Kuwait, Deputy Prime Minister Taha Yasin Ramadhan explained the decision in the following terms:

> How were we going to maintain the loyalty of the people and their support for the leader if they saw the inability of the leadership to provide a minimal standard of living in this rich country? In this situation, could you lead the army and the people in any battle, no matter what its level and under any banner? I think not. I am not deviating from my deep faith in victory in this battle, but whatever the outcome, if death is definitely coming to this people and this revolution, let it come while we are standing.[6]

In early 1990, oil prices dropped steeply from $20 per barrel to $13.70, causing great consternation in cash-strapped Iraq. Saddam placed the blame squarely on Kuwait's and the United Arab Emirates' (UAE) tendency to produce above their OPEC-set quotas, thus driving prices down. He also accused them of adopting these policies at the behest of the United States for the explicit purpose of undermining Iraq's economy. In a memorandum sent to the Arab League, Iraq asserted that Kuwait and the UAE were part of "an international scheme to glut the oil market with a quantity of oil that exceeded their quotas as fixed by OPEC," and that "a drop of one dollar in the price of a barrel of oil leads to a drop of one billion dollars in Iraqi revenues annually." It also asserted that Iraq owed nothing to the Arab Gulf countries for their assistance against Iran since

it constituted "only a small portion of the great cost borne by the
Iraqi economy and people who offered rivers of blood in defense of
pan-Arab sovereignty and dignity."[7] As the crisis heightened, Saddam
raised the stakes by demanding a major adjustment of the border,
a clear statement by Kuwaiti leaders forgoing all loans to Iraq, and
an agreement to extend Iraq a new aid package totaling $10 billion.
To add legitimacy to his demand for a shift in the border, he added
a new accusation: Saddam now claimed that Kuwait was not only
hurting the economy of Iraq through unfair pricing but also through
outright theft of Iraq's oil by drilling below the border to get at the
huge deposits of the southern Rumaila fields.

The question of OPEC prices has always been a thorny one. Historically, countries like Saudi Arabia, Kuwait, and the UAE favored
low, stable prices to dissuade oil consumers from investing in
alternative energy sources. These countries tended to have few
alternatives to oil and preferred policies geared toward extending oil
exports over time. In contrast, countries such as Iraq and Iran, with
a strong potential in sectors other than oil, tended to favor higher
prices to fund ambitious industrialization schemes not possible in
Saudi Arabia or Kuwait. After the war, Iraq felt even more pressed
to raise as much cash as possible for postwar recovery projects. To
resolve the conflict, OPEC minsters agreed to a system of quotas
to ensure that the market would not be flooded and that prices
remained at a reasonable level. In hindsight, it seems rather odd that
Kuwait was so brazen about its refusal to abide by OPEC quotas. In
1990, for example, before oil took a sharp drop, Kuwait's oil minister responded to accusations about overproduction by essentially
admitting it:

> First of all, I will tell you that we are producing above quota at the
> moment. Let us not beat about the bush on that. And I think that
> our obligation to stay within the quota applies when the price of the
> OPEC basket is below $18 per barrel and if the price is above $18
> per barrel, I think everyone should be producing above quota.[8]

Later he even declared his preference for scrapping the quota
system altogether. "From a practical standpoint," he added, "they
are already irrelevant, so that all that is needed is a recognition of

that fact."[9] For Saddam this was nothing short of economic warfare, and his response was unequivocal:

> I wish to tell those of our [Arab] brothers who do not seek war, and those who do not intend to wage war on Iraq, that we cannot tolerate this type of economic warfare which is being waged against Iraq. I believe that all our brothers know our situation and are informed about it and that, God willing, the situation will turn out well. But I say that we have reached a state of affairs where we cannot take the pressure. I believe we will all benefit and the Arab nation will benefit from the principle of adherence to OPEC resolutions on production and prices.[10]

Fears of a broader, foreign-orchestrated conspiracy were enhanced by increasing tensions with the army. As noted in Chapter 1, the Ba'ath Party was always wary of the military institution, and following its war with Iran, Iraq seemed ripe for a coup. The army, more than any other institution, felt cheated. Many senior officers privately blamed Saddam who repeatedly scolded his officers, ignored their advice, and, despite overwhelming advantages in arms and support, failed to score a decisive victory on an enemy weakened by internal divisions. Between 1988 and 1990, the country witnessed at least four failed coup attempts. Late in 1988 and again in 1989, around fifty officers were executed on charges of conspiracy to topple the regime. Hundreds of others, like Lieutenant-General Mahir 'Abdul-Rashid, the hero of the Fao battle, were sent into retirement. The most notable victim of these purges was Saddam's cousin and brother-in-law, the Minister of Defense General 'Adnan Khayrallah Tulfah, who died in a mysterious helicopter crash in 1989. He is almost uniformly described as the most capable man in the regime and enjoyed great popularity in the army. When I visited Baghdad in 2004 after the fall of Saddam's regime, I noticed that his was the only statue still standing in a Sunni neighborhood of Baghdad. It is widely believed that Saddam, unable to accuse him openly of betrayal, ordered his assassination. For a regime that placed its survival above all other considerations, it is not unrealistic to suppose that a decision to invade Kuwait, as well as seeking to gain what it felt to be legitimate rights, might have also considered the benefits of exporting its military crisis away from Baghdad.

These factors were all magnified by a naturally xenophobic regime which viewed increasing US criticisms of its WMD programs, and the collapse of several friendly East European regimes, as signs pointing toward an international conspiracy. As Iraq threatened, Kuwait seemed to grow more intransigent. Perhaps Kuwaiti leaders took Iraq's past commitments to non-aggression at face value. As recently as 1980, for example, Saddam had signed an Arab pledge toward "the renunciation of the use of force by any Arab country against another and the resolution of all inter-Arab disputes by peaceful means."[11] Or perhaps they felt that the international community, especially the US, would never stand for anything more than harmless saber-rattling. As for Saddam, if he had any worries about American reaction, these were apparently laid to rest just a few days before he finally ordered his tanks across the border. On 25 July, he summoned the US Ambassador April Glaspie to lay the matter before her. In the transcripts of the conversation Saddam stops just short of declaring his intention to invade, but he was clear enough: "when they [Kuwait and the United Arab Emirates] try to weaken Iraq, then they are helping the enemy. And then Iraq has the right to defend itself."[12] Rather than warning him of American and international responses to any acts of aggression, Ambassador Glaspie responded with some tame words: "I admire your extraordinary efforts to rebuild your country. I know you need funds. We understand that and our opinion is that you should have the opportunity to rebuild your country. But we have no opinion on the Arab–Arab conflicts, like your border disagreement with Kuwait."[13]

The last sentence was all that Saddam wanted to hear. Later, his Foreign Minister, Tariq Aziz, would reveal that they did expect some type of American response, but apparently not a major military strike. Yet anyone with even a rudimentary knowledge of the history of American interests in the region must surely have predicted what would happen in the event Iraq occupied Kuwait.

The United States and the Middle East

Concerted US involvement in the Middle East started only after the Second World War. After Europe, the Middle East witnessed the earliest instances of direct confrontations between the two postwar superpowers. Clashes over hegemonic influence grew violent in such places as Greece, Turkey, and Iran, leading President Truman to announce the first of several "doctrines" defining US policy in the Middle East. The Truman Doctrine allowed for financial and military aid to countries threatened with "communist aggression." The Cold War, however, was not the only issue of concern for the US. The creation of the state of Israel in 1948 received strong support in the US Congress with repeated declarations of special friendship and guarantees of assistance by all subsequent administrations. This commitment became even stronger after Israel's victory over Soviet-supported Egypt and Syria in the 1967 war. Most important of all, though, was America's great appetite for oil. Even before the Second World War, US oil corporations were active in Arabia, eventually coming together to form the ARAMCO partnership. American–Saudi relations were thus formed around a strong "pact" committed to fully integrating Saudi oil production with America's oil industry. America was quick to grasp one of nature's oddities in having over 65 percent of proven oil reserves of the world's foremost producers located in the Persian Gulf region. Such a concentration of the industrial world's most valuable commodity made oil

> the axiom of American Middle East policy as it has been since World War II. But it is more than that. Oil underpins America's global hegemony, America's policy in the Middle East was designed to make the United States the hegemonic power in the Gulf region as a prelude to a future veto over any challenge from any industrial competitor.[14]

This was more than evident in several events involving the US and the Middle East. During the 1950s, led by Egypt and Iran, a number of states in the region took steps, sometimes violently, to establish greater control over their national economies, including a greater say in oil production. This led President Eisenhower to issue another doctrine in 1957, authorizing direct American intervention, militarily if need be, if its "local allies" were threatened. This could include a domestic change of government. On one level, the Eisenhower Doctrine was aimed at Soviet incursions or communist takeovers. On another, however, it was motivated purely by a concern to maintain an unchallenged control over oil. That same year, the president wrote to one of his advisers: "I think you have, in the analysis presented in the letter, proved that should a crisis arise threatening to cut the Western world off from the Mid East oil, we would *have* to use force."[15] In this manner, the political foundation of US military intervention was already fully established long before Iraq's invasion of Kuwait. Should any further clarification be needed, this was provided by President Carter after the Iranian Revolution of 1979. In 1980, he issued the Carter Doctrine which specifically noted that American interests in the Gulf were so vital that the US reserved for itself the right to defend them unilaterally by force if necessary. For this very purpose the Rapid Deployment Force was created and later put to use against Iraq.

Invasion and defeat

Regardless of whether Saddam understood these matters or not, he was crystal clear on one thing: His regime was in deep trouble and the enemy was Kuwait. On 2 August 1990, without consulting his top officers, he ordered a massive invasion of the Emirate. The conquest was so rapid (only a few days), and so large (about 300,000 troops), that many expected a subsequent push into Saudi Arabia. The strong response of the United States and its allies represented the first major confrontation of the post-Cold War order. For the Americans, the prospect of having the oil of the Gulf in the hands of a single hostile regional power was unthinkable. This was also a clear opportunity to establish a permanent military presence in the area and settle the niggling matter of Iraq's WMD program. The first response came fast in the form of United Nations Resolution 661 which demanded an unconditional withdrawal and imposed on Iraq history's most comprehensive embargo. A flurry of Arab and international diplomatic efforts followed, all with the aim of convincing Saddam to withdraw. But now that the die had been cast, this was simply out of the question. In comments to a visiting Arab diplomat he said, "We have no guarantees if we withdraw. [...] Why should we withdraw at the last moment?"[16]

Saddam actually upped the ante by announcing the annexation of Kuwait. Iraqi radio declared that the "branch had returned to the stem" and that Kuwait would henceforth be known as Iraq's nineteenth province. In a vain effort to gain broad Arab support he tried to link Iraqi withdrawal from Kuwait with Israeli withdrawal from Palestinian territories and Syrian withdrawal from Lebanon. He also called for a conference to settle all the outstanding issues of the Middle East together. Such proposals were vehemently rejected by the US which now seemed eager to punish Iraq. Even after the bombing had started and when all avenues to success seemed closed, Saddam remained defiant. In discussions with a Soviet envoy who had urged him to withdraw, he said: "If America decided on war it will go to war whether I withdraw from Kuwait or not. They were conspiring against us. They were targeting the leadership for assassination. What have the Iraqis lost? They might yet gain!"[17]

In the meantime, the Kuwaitis, backed by American advisers, launched a far more sophisticated public relations effort. Worried that simply evoking international law would not swing the American public in favor of military action, they resorted to a variety of fabricated stories of supposed Iraqi atrocities. The most bizarre took place on the advice of Victor Clarke who was then representing one of the leading advertising agencies in Washington DC, and who was later given the post of Pentagon spokesman. Kuwait's ambassador to the US, Sa'ud al-Sabah, put forward his own daughter, who had not been in Kuwait throughout the ordeal, to give a fictitious testimony before Congress as an "ordinary" eyewitness to Iraqi soldiers supposedly stealing incubators and tossing infants on the floor.

The "Mother of All Battles," as Saddam called it, started when an American-led coalition of thirty-four countries, including Saudi Arabia, Egypt and Syria, launched a series of operations aimed at destroying Iraq's military might and driving it out of Kuwait. Despite the international nature of the coalition, it was dominated by the US which contributed over 75 percent of the troops. The first phase of the attack on Iraq started in January 1991, with a massive air bombardment. Over 116,000 sorties targeted not only Iraqi military formations, which would have been more than enough to secure victory, but also airports, bridges, roads, factories, communications centers, anything that looked like a depot, suspected homes of Ba'athist leaders; in short, the entire infrastructure of the country was laid to waste. Saddam's strategy was to dig in and hold on long enough for international and Arab public opinion to turn against the war and fragment the coalition. To this end he ordered several missile strikes against Israel in the hope that an Israeli reaction would turn the Arab world to his side. This plan failed when neither Israel nor the Arab world responded. Beyond several demonstrations, notably among the Palestinians, the Arab part of the coalition stood firm.

In February, the ground assault began and quickly turned into a rout of the Iraqi forces. Not only were retreating Iraqi troops gunned down mercilessly on the highway to Basra, but US forces also managed to occupy large parts of southeastern Iraq. Saddam committed one last crime before ordering a retreat when he ordered the torching of a number of Kuwaiti oil wells, resulting in an ecological disaster. Casualty numbers reveal that this was far from being a real contest. The Second Gulf War left anywhere between 10,000 to 63,000 Iraqi soldiers and around 1,000 to 5,000 civilians killed. Only 269 coalition troops died. Facing such losses it seemed as if the regime's days were numbered, especially when news filtered out of rebellions among the retreating troops. The Iraqi army was so thoroughly defeated that the road to Baghdad lay open. Rather than pursue Saddam, as some of his military commanders had urged, US President George Bush held back, giving Saddam the time and space to re-establish control over his remaining troops. Most of the Iraqi casualties were among the conscripted army rather than the elite Republican Guards units which were not thrown into the battle. They tended to be more loyal to the regime and held together in the face of growing rebelliousness. On 3 March, Iraqi military commanders signed the terms of the ceasefire. They included a recognition of Kuwaiti sovereignty, payment of reparations, acceptance of "no-fly" zones covering most of the country, full cooperation with United Nations inspectors charged with uncovering and destroying all of Iraq's WMD, and full compliance with a strict sanctions regime which essentially cut the country off from the rest of the world.

Uprising and consolidation

Throughout the Kuwait crisis, President Bush repeated a call to the people of Iraq to rid themselves of the Saddam regime. The most direct call came on 15 February 1991, as Iraqi troops retreated from Kuwait: "There is another way for the bloodshed to stop. And that is for the Iraqi military and the Iraqi people to take matters into their own hands and force Saddam Hussein, the dictator, to step aside."[18] In the meantime, he added, "there will be no cessation of hostilities, there will be no pause, there will be no cease-fire."[19] Thus, when a tank officer retreating from Kuwait turned his gun against a giant mural of Saddam on the outskirts of Basra, he and the multitudes who joined him had every reason to expect American assistance. The rebellion spread throughout the south and was eventually joined by Kurdish groups in the north as well. By mid-March, the regime was fighting for its life as practically every province outside Baghdad fell to rebel forces.

During the March Uprising, as it was called, rebels attacked Ba'athists and regime supporters in acts of uncontrolled vengeance, killing hundreds. It seemed as if Baghdad would soon witness a final showdown but for four factors that ultimately helped bring Saddam from the brink. First, the rebellion was completely spontaneous, lacking a recognized leadership. Rebel groups often remained ignorant of one another or were led by leaders hostile to one another. They generally did not coordinate their efforts, allowing Saddam's surviving forces to pick them off one by one. To a great extent this points to the feeble nature of the Iraqi opposition, which remained hopelessly divided by jealousies and ideologies. Second, though several groups, such as the communists and nationalists, did their best to give the uprising some direction, the most influential groups in the Shi'i south were the Iranian-backed Islamists. While all opposition groups suffered at the hands of the Ba'ath, the Shi'i parties were the only ones benefiting from a determined sponsor. Their alliance with Iran certainly reflected a sense of ideological fraternity, especially on the level of the leadership. But for most Iraqi Shi'is, who had fought so hard in the Iran war to maintain the independence of the country, such an alliance was viewed simply as a convenient source of aid during desperate times. Still, Shi'i groups, like the Badr Brigades of the Supreme Council for the Islamic Revolution in Iraq (SCIRI), often did more damage to their cause by inspiring fear of Iranian domination and sectarian strife, causing many neutrals to oppose the uprising. Third, as mentioned above, Saddam's Republican Guard units suffered hardly any serious losses during the war since they were pulled out of Kuwait and kept around Baghdad before the coalition's offensive. This force, composed mainly of Sunnis of rural backgrounds, remained loyal to the regime for fear that its collapse would lead to their ruin as well. These were the best equipped, best trained units in the Iraqi army and proved to be more than a match for the chaotic rebels. Lastly, America simply backed away from assisting the rebels. In a rather shameful about-face, Bush refused to aid the uprising on the grounds that the rebellion, with its populist bent and Iranian influence, could very well lead to the formation of a government that would not be to the liking of the US administration. America's allies in the region, notably Kuwait and Saudi Arabia, also warned against such an outcome and voiced their preference for a weakened and permanently contained Saddam rather than an unpredictable mass revolt. Despite all these weaknesses and the desperate state of the rebels after Saddam's counterattack, specifically sectarian slogans were rare as the focus remained firmly fixed on the removal of Saddam and the establishment of a representative government.

The result was horrible and predictable. After enforcing the no-fly agreement, American pilots were ordered to refrain from shooting at Saddam's helicopter gun-ships which were then used to cut down the insurgents. Rebels begged American soldiers, occupying land not far from the fighting, to let them have access to captured Iraqi weapons, but to no avail. Having been driven to the edge, Saddam did not hesitate to play the sectarian card to rally Sunnis around his crumbling regime. Up to this point, the regime's use of sectarianism was latent rather than overt, but as his troops approached the rebel-held city of Karbala, tanks could be seen painted with slogans such as, "No Shi'is After Today." Neither did commanders, such as Saddam's cousin Hussein Kamil, hesitate to order the bombing and partial destruction of sacred Shi'i shrines. The repression that followed was filmed by Iraqi officials for later use in training new security personnel. In one such film (probably intentionally leaked to magnify the fear), Ali Hasan al-Majid is shown brutalizing prisoners and declaring his intention to wipe out whole tribes in the south. Most of the mass graves containing tens of thousands later discovered in the south after the fall of the regime date back to this episode. Most of the religious colleges of Najaf and Karbala, which had boasted the cream of Shi'i scholarship, were closed and almost all of their teachers and students were killed, detained, or escaped into exile.

With the south subdued, Saddam's forces turned against the Kurds. Once again, the US, which was certainly in a position to prevent this massacre with minimal threat to its own troops, stood by and did nothing. With the Anfal campaign still fresh in their minds, panic ensued and up to half the population simply fled across the border to Turkey. Kurdish leaders, exasperated and angry at what they clearly saw as American betrayal, accepted Saddam's invitation to discuss peace terms. They agreed to lay down their arms in return for a renewed, albeit suspect, pledge to respect Kurdish autonomy, a general pardon, and permission for the return of the refugees. In the meantime, media coverage focusing on the plight of the Kurdish refugees (unlike events in the south which received almost no coverage) had had a strong effect on public opinion, pushing the US and Britain finally to step in. They implemented operation "Provide Comfort" whereby a no-fly zone in most of Iraqi Kurdistan was enforced and United Nations aid was allowed to flow in freely. Once the no-fly zone was enforced, government control in the north collapsed and the Kurdish groups took over. The Kurdish region has remained outside Baghdad's control since then. All in all, the March Uprising led to the death of between 30,000 to 60,000 in the south and at least 10,000, mostly refugees, in the north. Over 2 million Iraqis, about 8 percent of the population, were displaced. Politically, both Kurdish and Shi'i leaders had learned a terrible lesson about dealing with the US, and this would affect all their subsequent dealings.

Victory for whom?

Many observers in the West must have chuckled when they heard Saddam claim victory. There is, however, every reason to believe that the Iraqi dictator meant exactly what he said. For Saddam, the war was first and foremost about staying in power and this he achieved against all the odds. Not only did he defeat a serious uprising, but, more importantly, the Iraqi army which had been his main threat now lay in tatters. There were other changes as well. Notwithstanding his secular Arab nationalism, Saddam always dealt cautiously with the Shi'is, even after they had demonstrated their patriotism during the Iran war. In his mind, this lack of trust was confirmed after the March Uprising which he considered nothing short of treasonous. As a result there was a strong turn toward more overt sectarian favoritism. The war also resulted in a separation between the Kurdish and Arab regions of the country. The allied-protected Kurdish enclave now became self-governing and in the next decade a new generation of Kurds would grow up studying in Kurdish-language schools, free of Baghdad's control. Lastly, the war brought a new, large American military presence in the heart of the oil-rich Gulf.

From a broader Middle Eastern perspective, the war did not represent a qualitatively new development. Rather it was viewed as the latest in a series of imperialist interventions going back to the nineteenth century and aimed at thwarting the rise of an ambitious regional power. Hardly anyone in the region took seriously US claims that it was there to protect the sanctity of international law and the rights of small states. It was still an odd war in that the US and its allies actually made a hefty profit by charging Saudi Arabia, Kuwait, and the UAE around $84 billion for their services. The main differences between this war and past confrontations in the Middle East were the lack of a competing superpower on the one hand, and the nature of the Iraqi regime on the other. The latter issue, in particular, stood out as previous attempts by regional powers to challenge Western hegemony were usually accompanied by a level of significant popular support. Leaders such as Mossadeq of Iran and Nasser of Egypt had a broad base of support that genuinely believed in their nationalist ideals and promises of a better life ahead. The Arab nationalism of Saddam's Ba'ath had long since become a spent force after repeatedly failing to deliver that elusive goal of Arab unity. If anything, the regime's policies had actually accentuated inter-Arab divisions. Hopes that Saddam's dictatorship might yet improve living conditions were dealt a severe blow after two devastating wars and a decade of brutal repression. Rather than seeing this war as a heroic struggle for national liberation, most Iraqis considered it a disaster in which they were the unwilling victims of the terror of the dictatorship and the ruthlessness of imperialism. Both would grow even more vicious in the decade to come, with Iraqi citizens again paying the price.

4 | The sanctions regime

For the second time in only a couple of years, Iraq lay devastated after the end of a war. This time, however, the damage was far more serious. Unlike the Iran war, the bombardment was more intensive and affected the entire country, the subsequent civil war led to deeper social scars, and the establishment of a Kurdish enclave effectively partitioned the country. In the long run, however, the most damaging fallout of the Second Gulf War was the imposition of sanctions. The end of the Iran war brought with it feelings of anger and rebellion directed at the regime. This time, the burdens were so heavy that the overwhelming mood was one of hopelessness. The ineffective role of the opposition, the ruthless repression of the regime, and the callous attitude of the US toward Iraqi suffering, all combined to create an overpowering sense of social paralysis.

The structure of sanctions

The sanctions imposed after Iraq's invasion of Kuwait were unlike any others in their scope and duration. They included a ban on the importation of many items including books, journals, most medicines, seeds, farming tools, livestock, spare parts, and machinery. Iraq's assets were frozen and it was initially not allowed to sell any oil. Later, oil shipments were permitted but only in quantities so small that it was unable to purchase food at the prewar level. This was particularly painful in a country that had imported nearly 70 percent of its food prior to the war. After the ceasefire, the United Nations passed Resolution 687 which spelled out the conditions Iraq must meet in order to lift the sanctions. These included the complete destruction of all stockpiled chemical and biological weapons and their delivery systems, the dismantling of all WMD programs, the release of Kuwaiti prisoners, and the payment of war reparations estimated at over $100 billion. Compensation took the form of altering the border in favor of Kuwait, and setting aside 30 percent of oil revenues for reparations. A special "Compensation Fund" was created to handle the payments. In effect, Iraq lost much of its sovereignty either directly through border alterations and the creation of the Kurdish enclave, or through the lack of control over its own finances.

A few months after the end of the war, and partly as a result of real worries over a human calamity, the sanctions were modified a bit to allow Iraq to sell $1.6 billion of oil every six months on condition that the revenues be monitored to ensure that they were used for the purchase of humanitarian supplies. Saddam rejected this offer partly because he objected to excessive UN controls, but also because he felt that he might be able to hold on long enough for a better deal. By 1995, he received a better offer of $1 billion every three months. Initially this too was rejected but conditions had deteriorated, and hyperinflation was threatening complete economic collapse; as this would have affected even his own, partially insulated, supporters, Saddam reluctantly agreed.[1] The "Oil for Food" program, as it was called, came into effect by the end of 1996 bringing much-needed stability to the currency and supplies of food and some medicines. According to the UN Human Rights Rapporteur: "Had the Government of Iraq not waited five years to decide to accept the 'oil for food' agreement millions of innocent people would have avoided [...] suffering."[2]

That was clear enough, but the US and Britain were not completely free of blame either. When the sanctions were first imposed, US ideologues such as Anthony Lake advocated sanctions as a tool of containment rather than change.[3] But by the middle of the decade, the US began unilaterally to include a new condition of "regime change." This helped create discord within the UN and hampered the smooth management of the sanctions program, as France and Russia, among others, began to suspect any and all US and British initiatives. It also made Saddam more desperate and less likely to cooperate. Madeleine Albright, the American Ambassador to the UN, even insinuated that the sanctions could remain open-ended: "We do not agree that if Iraq complies with its obligations concerning weapons of mass destruction, sanctions should be lifted."[4] The US and Britain actually made a good profit from the deal because they were the chief importers of Iraqi oil at mandated below-market prices. Saddam also did his best to corrupt the process by bribing UN officials and a number of influential personalities around the world, allegedly including Benon Sevan, executive director of the program itself. Companies were encouraged to pay kickbacks to a secret account for the privilege of purchasing Iraqi oil at reduced prices or selling goods to Iraq at inflated prices. One study, conducted in 2003, estimated the overpricing on a number of contracts valued at $6.9 billion to have been as high as $656 million. In 2001, the captain of the oil tanker *Essex* confessed to making arrangements to smuggle out $10-million-worth of Iraqi oil.

The UN established ten separate bodies to enforce and administer, at Iraq's expense, the various parts of the "sanctions regime." One of the most important was the UN Special Commission (UNSCOM) charged with the difficult task of finding and eliminating Iraq's WMDs and the programs that produced them. From the moment it started its work in 1991 until 1997 when it was expelled by Iraq, it uncovered a massive program which included forty nuclear research centers, and numerous factories producing thousands of chemical munitions. UNSCOM's task was made more difficult since Baghdad did everything short of outright force to impede or sabotage its work. Saddam was not only concerned about losing his beloved weapons but also because there was clear evidence that parts of UNSCOM were being used as a vehicle for US espionage. He grew even more suspicious when the US moved the goal posts with its insistence on regime change. In 1997, he halted all cooperation and closed down UNSCOM's offices. Once the team left Iraq, the US and Britain initiated an intensive bombing campaign which reached an average of one strike every third day for the next several years; this, despite it being clear to most of those involved that UNSCOM had fulfilled its job and that Iraq was now free of WMD. Scott Ritter, one of the chief UN weapons inspectors, had this to say when asked about the potential threat from Iraq: "No one has backed up any allegations that Iraq has reconstituted WMD capability with anything that remotely resembles substantive fact,"[5] and, "if I had to quantify Iraq's threat, I would say [it is] zero."[6]

The social cost

If the two previous wars had inflicted major damage on Iraqi society, then the thirteen years of sanctions initiated the unraveling of its very fabric. In a country often envied for its riches, over 70 percent of the population was below the poverty line and 60 percent became directly dependent on aid for their very survival. The decade of the 1990s witnessed an alarming deterioration in overall nutrition, health, and infant mortality. According to a 1999 UN report on Iraq:

> Iraq's GDP may have fallen by nearly two-thirds in 1991, owing to an 85 percent decline in oil production and the devastation of the industrial services sectors of the economy. Per capita income fell from $2,279 US dollars in 1984 to $627 in 1991 and [...] less than $700 in 1998. Other sources estimate a decrease in per capita GDP to be as low as $450 US dollars in 1995.[7]

Such a drop, accompanied by large-scale damage to infrastructure, directly affected nutrition so that by 1995 dietary energy intake had fallen by two-thirds of its prewar levels. Between 1991 and 1996, malnutrition doubled in children under five years old. The damage done to the country's electricity plants also affected the water purification systems. And if that were not enough, the Sanctions Committee consistently blocked the importation of chlorine on the grounds that it might be used in the manufacture of chemical weapons. Contaminated water, malnutrition, and a general decline in healthcare resulted in disturbingly high mortality rates, especially among children. Between 1984 and 1989, there were 56 infant deaths per 1,000 live births. By 1995–2000, that rate had climbed to 131 deaths. Many of these deaths were due to dysentery, a direct result of water contamination. The callousness with which some of these issues were handled seems simply unbelievable. Children's vaccines, against diphtheria and yellow fever, for example, were banned because, as an official in the British government explained, "they are capable of being used in weapons of mass destruction."[8] Estimates vary as to the number of children who died as a direct result of the sanctions from 200,000 to well over half a million. UN estimates made in 1997 state that, as a result of the scarcity of medical supplies, about one-third of hospital beds were no longer used, three-quarters of their medical equipment was not functioning and one-quarter of the country's health clinics were closed. The deterioration of the healthcare system also came about as a result of a "brain-drain" as doctors, along with many qualified professionals in general, fled the country. The Ba'athist regime had started this trend back in 1980 when over forty medical specialists were expelled for political reasons. By the 1990s, the shortage of physicians was so acute that some of the lecturers at Baghdad's once famous Medical School had only a Bachelor's degree. By 2003, as much as 15 percent of the population had left the country.

The education system, which was one of the best in the region, also suffered in a variety of ways. Emigration of qualified teachers again played a role, as did the dreaded Sanctions Committee which blocked the importation of almost all scientific journals and books. UN inspectors then went through Iraqi libraries and ordered the destruction of many materials on the grounds, again, that they might be used in Saddam's now non-existent WMD program. Lack of funds and the inability to import spare parts closed many factories which used to produce materials such as pencils and notebooks. As a result, literacy, which had been as high as 80 percent (some claim up to 90 percent) before the war, had dropped to 58 percent by 2003.

It is quite likely that the extensive use of depleted uranium (DU) had much to do with the reportedly rising cancer rates and birth defects, especially in the south. After all these years, no systematic studies have been undertaken on this potentially catastrophic subject. What is known is that well over 300 metric tonnes of DU were dropped on Iraq during the war. Despite concerns over its possible long-term impact on health, the US military insists on its use because it remains relatively cheap and very effective in piercing armor. Iraq's own cancer specialists complained repeatedly of the problem to Western reporters, as in this account given in 2000:

> Our own studies indicate that more than 40 per cent of the population in this area will get cancer: in five years' time to begin with, then long afterwards. Most of my own family now have cancer, and we have no history of the disease. It has spread to the medical staff of this hospital. We don't know the precise source of the

contamination, because we are not allowed to get the equipment to conduct a proper scientific survey, or even to test the excess level of radiation in our bodies. We suspect depleted uranium, which was used by the Americans and British in the Gulf War right across the southern battlefields.[9]

Unlike Kuwait, the contaminated areas in Iraq were left untreated since the needed equipment was blocked by the Sanctions Committee as were the drugs and medical equipment required to treat cancer. In fact, by 2002 there were an estimated $5-billion-worth of contracts on hold supposedly because of their potential military use. Many UN officers on the ground in Iraq battled heroically to draw attention to the matter. Dr Karol Sikora, for example, of the UN's World Health Organization, complained that the "requested radiotherapy equipment, chemotherapy drugs and analgesics are consistently blocked by United States and British advisers [to the Sanctions Committee]. There seems to be a rather ludicrous notion that such agents could be converted into chemical or other weapons."[10] The most high-profile case was of Denis Halliday, the coordinator of humanitarian relief to Iraq and Assistant Secretary-General of the United Nations. In 1998, he handed in his resignation note which stated: "I am resigning because the policy of economic sanctions is totally bankrupt. We are in the process of destroying an entire society. It is as simple and terrifying as that [...] Five thousand children are dying every month [...] I don't want to administer a programme that results in figures like these."[11] Those who remained grew bolder in condemning what was clearly a form of collective punishment. One particularly stinging UN paper went as far as to suggest a deliberate policy of genocide:

> The sanctions regime against Iraq has as its clear purpose the deliberate infliction on the Iraqi people of conditions of life (lack of adequate food, medicines, etc.) calculated to bring about its physical destruction in whole or in part. It does not matter that this deliberate physical destruction has as its ostensible objective the security of the region. Once clear evidence was available that thousands of civilians were dying and that hundreds of thousands would die in the future as the Security Council continued the sanctions,

the deaths were no longer an unintended side effect – the Security Council was responsible for all known consequences of its actions. The sanctioning bodies cannot be absolved from having the "intent to destroy" the Iraqi people.[12]

Hardest hit was Iraq's once large and comfortable salaried middle class. Hyperinflation reduced average incomes to the impossible level of $3–$10 per month. Overall, by the mid-1990s the average purchasing power of Iraqi families dropped to only 5 percent of what it had been prior to the sanctions. The state also cut back on many services and imposed fees on those that were previously free, including medical care. After using most of their savings and selling off household items, people started looking for second and third jobs. Iraqi newspapers were full of such stories, like that of the schoolteacher Buthayna Jabbar, whose monthly salary of 100 dinars had been sufficient to pay the rent and buy food. During the sanctions she was forced to sell trinkets in the street while her husband (also a salaried employee) worked as a laborer after hours.[13] The problem was not limited to physical hardships but also had a direct impact on the deterioration of moral values that bind society. Divorce rates climbed as couples struggled to manage their lives, as did the number of homeless and beggars in the streets. Prostitution, corruption at all levels, smuggling, and violent crime rose dramatically in what was previously a safe country. Iraqis were suddenly introduced to the new phenomenon of powerful mafia groups, some with ties to the government elite. Turf wars grew more common and the new atmosphere of cut-throat competition led to serious clashes between gangs led by different Ba'athist officials. One such case showed that even the ruling family was not immune from fractious infighting. In 1995, Hussein Kamil, Saddam's cousin, son-in-law and former Minister of Military Industries, fled to Jordan as a result of a feud with Saddam's son 'Uday. He later returned on promises of clemency but was killed in a shootout with 'Uday's men. In 1996, 'Uday himself faced an assassination attempt which left him partially paralyzed. While the government press complained about the growing crime rate, there is every reason to believe that it actually benefited the regime by diverting scarce resources to its supporters:

A flourishing black market via the UAE, Iran and Turkey serves to foster a network of powerful interests running from the sons of influential figures (headed by Saddam's son Udai) to merchants, sanctions-profiteers and intermediaries. The lesser beneficiaries include intelligence officers, special Republican Guard members, truck drivers, retail traders and money changers. [...] [G]iven the regime's social structure, the sanctions' main impact was to empower the already powerful and impoverish the victims and opponents of the regime.[14]

Even the army, that once powerful institution, decimated by wars, Saddam's terror, and now the sanctions, was reduced to the same pitiful state as the rest of society. Faleh Abdul Jabar, an Iraqi writer, aptly described the condition of the officer corps in 1998:

Once feared and respected for their power – which in turn breeds wealth – they (the officer corps) have now sunk into dire need, along with large sections of the salaried middle class which has seen its income eroded by hyperinflation. Even colonels are now using over-crowded buses rather than their khaki-painted limousines. In the market place, officers bargain to get third-rate tomatoes.[15]

As if to rub salt into the wounds of Iraq's suffering multitudes, both Saddam and the US demonstrated a remarkable lack of concern. Saddam authorized a new spending spree to rebuild his numerous statues and murals, and for the construction of over twenty new grotesquely lavish palaces. In 1994, he opened the new 300-foot-high Saddam International Tower, and started construction on the mammoth "Mother of All Battles" mosque, planned to be one of the largest of its kind in the world. On the other hand, Madeleine Albright's interview on CBS only confirmed Iraqis' worst fears about US intentions:

[CBS's] LESLEY STAHL: " [...] We have heard that a half a million children have died. I mean that's more children than died in Hiroshima. And, you know, is the price worth it?"

MADELEINE ALBRIGHT: "I think this is a very hard choice, but the price – we think the price is worth it. [...] It is a moral question. But the moral question is even a larger one. Don't we owe to the

American people and to the American military and to the other
countries in the region that this man not be a threat?"

STAHL: "Even with the starvation and the lack ..."

ALBRIGHT: "I think, Lesley – it is hard for me to say this because I
am a humane person, but my first responsibility is to make sure
that United States forces do not have to go and re-fight the Gulf
War."[16]

The Kurdish region

The UN-mandated "no-fly" zone in the north allowed Kurdish
nationalist groups to establish an area of control beyond Baghdad's
reach. This, however, did not immediately bring stability to the area.
Having been left unprotected while Saddam's planes rained chemical weapons and destroyed their villages, few felt safe. In addition,
Turkish incursions into northern Iraq looking for their own Kurdish rebels increased this sense of insecurity. And, like their Arab
counterparts, the Kurds were also affected by the sanctions. Iraqi
Kurdistan, in fact, suffered from a double embargo, one by the UN
and the other by Baghdad. The most destructive factor, though,
was the intense hostility between the two main Kurdish groups,
the Kurdistan Democratic Party (KDP) and the Patriotic Union of
Kurdistan (PUK). Both have their roots in the post-Second World
War period of Iraq. In 1946, a number of leading Iraqi Kurdish
personalities, led by the now legendary Mullah Mustafa Barzani,
formed the KDP. Their goal was to push, in a variety of ways, for
Kurdish national rights in Iraq, including the right of self-govern-
ance. For the next ten years it remained rather isolated. The 1958
Revolution brought about a growth in political activism throughout
Iraq and, as a result, the KDP quickly developed into a prominent
organization. As it grew, competing tendencies appeared within its
ranks, reflecting a number of issues. Ideologically, disagreements
arose over the question of independence and whether the party
should embrace socialism. Factions tended to be divided by region
(Irbil versus Sulaymania), social background (urban versus rural),
and religious convictions.[17] Jalal Talbani, a highly urbane intellectual
from a family of Qadiriyya sheikhs, lashed out at the "feudalist tribal"
leadership of the Naqshabandi Mullah Mustafa Barzani.

In 1961, disagreements with Baghdad over the nature and extent of Kurdish national rights (which were officially recognized), led to the outbreak of violence and rebellion. Kurdish armed rebellion continued until 1975 when it suffered a crushing blow dealt by the Ba'ath. During this period, the KDP faced several splits which, after 1975, led to the establishment of the PUK under the leadership of Talbani. For a while, it seemed as if the PUK would become the leading Kurdish force as Mullah Mustafa grew ill and later died in exile. His sons, especially Mas'ud Barzani, eventually succeeded in reorganizing the KDP along more modern party lines. By the late 1970s, both parties began to re-establish guerrilla networks in the mountains of the north, though they tended to clash more among themselves than against government troops. The Iran–Iraq War gave the Kurdish rebellion a new lifeline, as most of the Iraqi army moved to the front and assistance was now made available from Iran. The KDP adopted a more pro-Iranian strategy during the war with the aim of overthrowing the regime, while the PUK, whose main support base bordered Iran and thus feared its domination, tried to negotiate a favorable deal with Saddam. These differing approaches, when added to their old rivalry, often led to serious conflict bordering on all-out civil war in Kurdistan. By 1988, it became clear to all that Saddam was no longer on the defensive and that the end of the war would surely bring an attack from Baghdad. The two parties, along with six other groups including the Iraqi Communist Party, reluctantly joined in the formation of the Iraqi Kurdistan Front.

The Front survived the ordeal of the Anfal campaign and after the Gulf War the US encouraged all sides to form the Kurdistan regional government. By this time, the KDP and the PUK were facing a serious rival in the Iranian-supported Islamic Movement of Kurdistan. Its fiery leader accused the PUK "of 30 years of corruption, deviation and fratricide in northern Iraq" and of assisting "Westerners [to] spread HIV viruses in Iraq's Kurdistan." He went on to declare that their "aim [was] to establish an Islamic state in northern Iraq similar to the one in Iran."[18] In 1992, general elections were held yielding a parliament divided exactly evenly between the KDP and PUK, and raising questions about the integrity of the voting passes. The new Kurdish regional government announced its intention of forming a federal union with Arab Iraq. This replaced the old demand for "autonomy" and placed greater emphasis on independence without going as far as complete secession. At this point, however, the Kurdish government was nothing short of a sham. Essentially, the two parties simply decided to divide the Kurdish region into two halves with the PUK governing the eastern half from Sulaymaniya and the KDP governing the western half from Irbil. Such an arrangement, while it did offer a temporary truce, failed to establish genuine reconciliation.

As the sanctions took hold, rivalries over scarce resources surfaced once again. Both parties actively engaged in smuggling and vied with one another over controlling the lucrative customs revenues from the trade with Turkey and Iran. Smuggling was controlled by specific party commanders and tribal leaders using their new-found revenues to broaden networks of patronage. As with the rest of the country, the sanctions accentuated class divisions and left the vast majority impoverished and helpless. Kurdistan was, however, better off in not having to endure regular air strikes and having greater access to international aid. Still, past animosities coupled with new rivalries, stirred up occasionally by Baghdad and neighboring states, all led to open clashes as early as 1993 and gradually escalated into full-fledged civil war lasting from 1994 to 1997. One NGO worker put it this way: "Barzani thinks he's the true leader of the Kurds. So does Talbani and they'll fight each other down to their last *peshmerga* [Kurdish guerrilla] to prove themselves right."[19] Saddam made especially good use of this conflict as he offered his services to Barzani and re-established a presence in Irbil. In 1997, worried about Saddam's growing influence, the US moved in more forcefully to mediate a settlement, and the following year the two parties agreed to return to the formula of territorial division and the sharing of customs revenues.

Survival strategies

Facing such horrendous problems, both state and society developed various strategies for survival. Saddam adopted the tried method of using violence and terror to control the resources and rewarding the one million people he believed were needed to keep his regime in power. Rather than working to fix the problems, he chose to manage and contain the developing chaos. Some measures, like cutting off the ears and noses of supposed criminals, raised the level of terror to new heights.[20] Organizationally, the security of the regime's inner core was bolstered through a series of "circles" of defense. The central circle was composed of an imposing presidential complex (today's American "Green Zone"), with the surrounding neighborhoods reserved for loyal security guards and their families. The next circle was comprised of the well-guarded neighborhoods where the top government officials lived, followed by lower-ranked officials. By establishing such clearly demarcated areas around the presidential complex, it was easier to defend the regime and also easier to keep an eye on the regime's elite. The period of sanctions witnessed a proliferation of overlapping and often competing security organizations with various names such as Fada'yi Saddam and the Quds Army. Baghdad's Shi'i areas were the chief sources of opposition, especially the huge slum of one million people known as Revolution City and renamed Saddam City.[21] After the 1991 uprising, Saddam stationed an elite battalion of Republican Guards nearby with instructions to close it off and bombard it indiscriminately in case of revolt.

To make sure the regular army stayed loyal, Saddam intensified past practices of rotation of officers, purges and the creation and re-creation of parallel military structures. Excessive terror, such as the 1999 execution of twenty-four senior officers, often strained relations with the officers' powerful Sunni tribes. To further protect himself, a new small elite praetorian guard was created in 1995. The Special Republican Guards, as they were called, were placed under the direct command of Saddam's younger and more capable son, Qusay, and charged specifically with protecting the president and fighting coups. Their members were drawn almost exclusively from Saddam's Al Bu Nasir tribe. As a sign of the utter contempt in which he held the regular army, Saddam finally broke with tradition and began appointing men, such as his cousins Hussein Kamil and Ali Hasan al-Majid, to the post of Minister of Defense even though they had absolutely no military background.

His most desperate method of surviving the sanctions was the now completely frank use of sectarianism. While it is true that the

Ba'ath Party's leadership has almost always been dominated by Sunni Arabs, its ideology continued to laud Arab nationalism above sectarian divides. Yet now that the regime had its back to the wall, it shifted to a policy of narrow sectarianism and the establishment of a tribal hierarchy with Saddam's immediate family on top. After years of condemning tribalism as a threat to national cohesion, Saddam established an official Assembly of Tribes and granted these resurrected tribes specific authority over such matters as limited revenue collection and law enforcement. Long-forgotten practices like honor-killing and the payment of blood money were given sanction. These measures benefited the regime by dividing any possible opposition, delegating some of the government's reduced power and creating a stronger sense of solidarity at the top among Saddam's inner circle. Tribal hierarchy was expressed through favoritism in granting government contracts, appointments and gifts. In general, Sunni tribes, of which Iraq has about ten large confederations, were favored. Within this group, those that demonstrated strong loyalty, such as the Dulaym, Jubur and 'Ubayd, were rewarded with appointments in the Republican Guards and the security services, and given a monopoly over smuggling lucrative items. Membership in the security services brought with it, in addition to power and contacts, real material benefits denied to the rest of the population: a free plot of land, home construction grants, and access to building materials, electronics, and food at discounted prices. Family members received free healthcare at elite military hospitals. "Re-tribalization" also carried with it various contradictions. These new tribes, unlike their predecessors, were completely dependent on the state, and their sheikhs were not always popular. By relinquishing power in some areas, the state risked competition and clashes with the tribes. Saddam rarely missed an opportunity to remind the sheikhs that their gains had come from his good graces. Now that scarcity was biting hard, his regime was the first to face the blame.

To combat the debilitating effects of the sanctions on the general population, the regime began issuing ration cards under the supervision of the UN. The ration card became another source of control as it required registration in a central databank and prevented the mobility of card holders. Also, the regime was able to hand out extra cards to its supporters. Distribution was channeled in a variety of ways to favored regions of the country, notably Baghdad and the Sunni Triangle, and to punish those who had rebelled in 1991. Here, whereas food and medicine distribution was monitored (to an extent) by the UN, reconstruction was not. So as the regime show-cased its ability to rebuild bridges and repair the electricity grid in Baghdad, the Shi'i south was left to rot. This was not merely due to the scarcity of resources since no funds were spared to carry out the massive project of draining the southern marshes as a way of punishing their inhabitants.

Beyond this, Saddam used the humanitarian crisis in an increas-ingly sophisticated propaganda war aimed at turning Arab and inter-national opinion against the sanctions. The government showed a new flexibility in allowing international coverage of scenes of mass suffering, and relevant statistics, normally a state secret, were made readily available. Gradually, the image of Iraq changed from one of an aggressor to that of a victim of rapacious Western imperialism. The coverage had a strong impact in the Arab world where donations were collected and embargo-busting planes started regular flights from Jordan, Syria, and Lebanon. Diplomatically, Iraq's relations improved with the Arab countries as relations were restored with Saudi Arabia in 2002 and friendly contacts with Kuwait took place. A decade after the sanctions were instituted, it appeared that the international consensus on maintaining them was breaking up, much to the consternation of Britain and the US whose diplomats used every means, legal and illegal, to prolong them. In 1999, an American official at the UN said: "The longer we can fool around in the [Security] Council and keep things static, the better."[22]

Society's means of coping

On the social front, people resorted to measures, both practical and psychological, to help them weather the storm without directly challenging the regime. The main avenue for most was to fall back on sub-national or primary forms of association such as family, clan, and the neighborhood mosque. The wave of religious revival that had affected the entire Middle East also left its mark on Iraq with a visible rise in people regularly praying and fasting, and an increase in the numbers of women wearing the Islamic veil. Mosques and Husayniyat (Shi'i religious centers) provided psychological comfort and acted as institutions of social support. Sheikh 'Ayyash al-Kubaysi, one of the leading Sunni religious leaders, referring back to this period, said that a whole new generation of young men were "reared in the mosque [... and] the mosque embraced them."[23] Even the regime tried to gain something from this religious mood by issuing a call for a "return to Islam."

An atmosphere of sectarianism and rising religious observances certainly assisted the underground Islamist groups at the expense of secular nationalists and communists. The most important Sunni figure was Muhammad Ahmad al-Rashid, a prolific writer and member of the Muslim Brothers who called on his followers to be patient and prepare for the coming battle with the regime. Some Shi'i leaders, for example Ayatollah Sistani, already one of the senior clerics at this time, urged caution and self-help, adopting a "quietist" approach on political matters. Others, like SCIRI and the Da'wa, had a more militant inclination and benefited from generous Iranian support. But the most interesting (and possibly most important in the long run) phenomenon was the emergence of the so-called "Sadr Movement" around the charismatic and daring Shi'i religious leader Muhammad Sadiq al-Sadr, sometimes called Sadr II in reference to the founder of the Da'wa Party discussed in Chapter 2. He had been something of a firebrand cleric for most of his life. First imprisoned in 1972, he earned strong support, especially among urban poor Shi'is, for his focus on assisting the needy and adopting a simple lifestyle. During the late 1960s and 1970s, he befriended the exiled Ayatollah Khomeini who was then living in Najaf and became an enthusiastic adherent of political activism as a means of establishing an Islamic state.

In 1991, he supported the uprising and ended up in one of Saddam's prisons. Upon his release he put his considerable energy into community work focusing on the slums of Baghdad. There he established independent Shi'i courts, set up soup kitchens, and organized youth into unarmed neighborhood defense units. He gained wide popularity and respect for his willingness to challenge the authorities openly by forbidding membership in the Ba'ath Party, refusing to mention Saddam's name during the Friday prayers,[24] and publicly praising Khomeini's views on Islamic government. His views were not all directed at the regime. Sadr II was also known as a strong advocate of conservative Islamic norms, including his insistence on female veiling even for Christians. He condemned Western culture and warned that the sanctions were part of imperialism's attack on Islam in general. In one of his talks he chastised his followers for listening to Western music or wearing American clothes: "Why do you imitate the West, when they try to subject you to their monopoly?"[25] His relationship with other religious leaders was often acrimonious since he criticized men like Sistani for remaining silent in the face of tyranny. Tolerated up to a point, the regime eventually could not ignore his rising popularity and increasingly bold speeches.

In may ways, the emergence of the Sadr Movement is partially due to the collapse of the Soviet Union and the resultant retreat of communist parties throughout the Middle East. In Iraq, the Sadrists now came to articulate a language emphasizing the plight of the poor and dispossesed, albeit with a strong sectarian bent. And today, the masses of people from the slums of Baghdad who make up the base of the movement are the very children of those that supported the Communist Party in the 1950s and 1960s. In 1999, Sadr II was assassinated along with two of his sons. After a brief period of confusion his many followers and organizations slowly came under the management of his surviving son Muqtada, who would emerge as a formidable leader in post-Saddam Iraq.

Regime consolidation and social collapse

By the end of the decade, Iraq had sunk from one of the wealthiest countries in the developing world to one of the poorest with child mortality, malnutrition and general economic indicators reaching levels akin to those of sub-Saharan Africa. As late as 2000, a UN report on the effects of sanctions was full of warnings:

> The sanctions against Iraq are the most comprehensive, total sanctions that have ever been imposed on a country. The situation at present is extremely grave. The transportation, power and communication infrastructures were decimated during the Gulf war,

and have not been rebuilt owing to the sanctions. The industrial sector is also in shambles and agricultural production has suffered greatly. But most alarming is the health crisis that has erupted since the imposition of the sanctions. [...] The sanctions upon Iraq have produced a humanitarian disaster comparable to the worst catastrophes of the past decades.[26]

But the situation, while not improving, was beginning to level off. Child mortality and malnutrition stabilized, and smuggling kept scarcity within semi-manageable levels. In 1999, the UN agreed to lift the ceiling on Iraqi oil exports, though this did not lead to major changes since the country's export capacity was still handicapped by infrastructural damage. By the late 1990s, Saddam was beginning to sound defiant once again, showing all the signs of a leader who had succeeded in saving his regime, albeit at the expense of his own society. It seemed increasingly clear that the US policy of regime change through sanctions had failed, and the mood in Washington was now shifting toward more drastic action. As talk of new options to "remove Saddam" grew, few seemed concerned about the consequences. Wars and sanctions had indeed left the regime weak, isolated, and with a base of support narrower than ever before. But they had also created a society suffering from a ruined economy and deep divisions, making it singularly ill-prepared to handle a fall of government, even one as despised as that of Saddam.

5 | Occupation and chaos

The new millennium saw two important developments that would set Iraq on the path toward American occupation. First, Saddam's tyranny and the oppressive sanctions regime combined to sap the country of its strength without weakening the regime's hold on power. This greatly disturbed many in Washington's corridors of power who felt that the US should have marched on Baghdad in 1991. On the other hand, it presented an enticing opportunity since a military invasion and occupation of Iraq would be much easier now that the sanctions had left the country with almost no defensive capabilities. Second, the change in the US administration with the assumption of George W. Bush Jr and his team of so-called "neo-conservative" ideologues who were quite eager to impose American will directly through the use of force. The result was the American invasion and occupation of the country in 2003. But America's decision to decapitate the Iraqi state without bothering to invest the large resources needed to rebuild it, created the conditions for chaos and a wholly sectarian atmosphere.

American views on Iraq

In Chapter 4, we reviewed America's strategic thinking toward the Middle East with specific focus on the importance of oil. Concerning Iraq at the end of the 1990s, policy-makers in the US and Britain were gradually coming to the conclusion that "regime change" through sanctions and active containment had failed. At the same time, they remained convinced that Saddam Hussein, though much weakened, continued to pose a threat to regional stability and American interests in the Middle East. In the meantime, other changes took place which encouraged the US to adopt a more forceful interventionist posture. The collapse of the Soviet Union and the problems of transition facing Russia meant the US now enjoyed an unprecedented window of opportunity to impose a new order in the Middle East to better suit American interests. Reports from Iraq indicated that while the regime was still strong enough to suppress revolts and palace coups, its military had grown so weak that it was unable to offer much resistance to an American-led invasion. More importantly, the United States witnessed a change in administration with a radically new foreign agenda. While it is not the chief goal of this work to dwell on the nature of US politics, a brief word on this issue is in order. Going back to the late 1980s, a number of American academics and policy-makers (especially prominent in the Pentagon) began to articulate a new role for the US in the post-Cold War world. Men like Dick Cheney, Donald Rumsfeld, Richard Perle, Paul Wolfowitz, and Zalmay Khalil-zad were also strongly influenced by American involvement in the Second Gulf War of 1990–91. They felt deeply disappointed that the US did not press the war further to ensure the removal of Saddam's regime and the installation of a new pro-American government in Iraq. In the words of Khalilzad, America's future ambassador in Iraq: "I remember sending memos to [Defense Secretary] Cheney, saying, 'You can't stop! We have an opportunity to do a bigger thing.' [...] there was this sense that we had not done the right thing in Iraq. We had unfinished business."[1]

In a way, the collapse of the Soviet Union and the hostility to Saddam were intimately linked, since Saddam suddenly emerged as the most visible symbol of defiance in the post-Cold War world. There is little doubt that Iraq's possession of the world's second largest oil reserves, situated in the middle of the oil-rich Gulf region, also influenced this thinking. The neo-conservatives' ideas were best articulated in the Pentagon's draft Defense Planning Guidance document of 1992. According to Khalilzad, one of its authors: "The central core of the D.P.G. was that bipolarity had ended, and the US was now the world's single leading power, and that our goal in this new era was to preclude a return to a bipolar system, or to a multipolar system."[2] One way of doing this was to prevent the emergence of dominant regional powers; something that could be accomplished through a more aggressive unilateralist posture of "pre-emptive war" against states perceived as hostile to the US. With respect to the Middle East, and the Arab countries in particular, the neo-conservatives viewed these as "artificial" countries which had no real histories of independence. Furthermore, they represented "failed" states which could be saved only through US intervention.

There is good evidence that the neo-conservatives set out to target Iraq immediately upon Bush's victory in the US elections. It was seen as the weak link in a Middle East in urgent need of a cure. Not only was it weak as a result of the sanctions, but a case could be made against Iraq in particular because of the unsavory nature of Saddam's regime and its record of regional aggression. Little mention was made of the US's previously strong support for Saddam during his war on Iran. An Iraq in American hands, it was thought, would become a base from which the US could project its power more effectively throughout the Middle East to help bring about fundamental transformations to the region as a whole. The most important transformations include the adoption of free market reforms and political liberalization. Exactly how this, especially liberalization, was supposed to take place in a socially complex region by a power (the US) which had so often supported authoritarian regimes over internal democratic impulses, remained unsaid.

On September 11, 2001, these plans received more urgency after the al-Qa'ida bombings in New York and Washington, DC. The subsequent American-led invasion of Afghanistan, which received broad international support because it specifically targeted al-Qa'ida, failed to detract from the administration's determination to attack Iraq. In fact, the very next day following the bombings, military leaders were ordered to draw up plans for the invasion of Iraq. To convince the US and international public opinion of the legitimacy of such a drastic action, the American administration launched a concerted yet ultimately shabby public relations campaign. The campaign focused on three points: (i) that, despite the work of the United Nations, Iraq still possessed weapons of mass destruction; (ii) that Iraq had strong ties with al-Qa'ida operatives; and (iii) that removing Saddam and his regime would usher in a period of peace, prosperity, and freedom for Iraq and the region as a whole. It is well known today that the first two arguments were erroneous and very likely to have been intentionally fabricated,[3] while the last would have required huge commitments in troops, monetary investments, and expertise, none of which was forthcoming. Nevertheless, in fall 2002, at the request of the US, the United Nations Security Council passed Resolution 1441 calling on Iraq to allow the return of UN inspectors and warning that it would face "serious consequences" if it obstructed their work. Facing such pressures Iraq agreed. The new United Nations Monitoring, Verification and Inspection Commission (UNMOVIC), and the International Atomic Energy Agency (IAEA), were granted even broader rights than the old UNSCOM team, including the right to inspect without notice any facility whatsoever (including private homes) and interview any individual "inside or outside the country [...] without the presence of observers from the Iraqi government."[4] Much to the annoyance of the American administration, both UNMOVIC and IAEA reported that they had found no evidence of any WMD or any program to reproduce them. In point of fact, none of the numerous US intelligence agencies (the CIA, Defense Intelligence, State Department and others) found any evidence to support the Bush administration's claims.

This lack of evidence did not deter Washington from pressing its cause in the most vocal and urgent manner. Yet, with all its considerable resources, the US was unable to win support for military action from its usual allies with the notable exception of Britain and Kuwait. Unlike the coalition of 1990, France, Germany, Russia, and China stood firm in their opposition to the call for invasion. Within the Middle East, even such strong US allies as Turkey, Egypt, and Saudi Arabia refused to back the American position. All the major international organizations, including the United Nations, NATO, and the European Union, suffered serious divisions and, at one point, even appeared to be on the brink of collapse. Fear of aggressive American neo-imperialism was one factor. The other was the competition over Iraq's oil. During the decade of the sanctions, Saddam had signed a number of long-term oil contracts with several countries, in particular Russia and France. French companies such as Total Fina Elf were allowed to exploit the country's huge untapped oil reserves under very favorable terms. This certainly affected the conflicting political views, with France and Russia favoring methods of gentle persuasion and prodding in a long-term effort to push the Iraqi regime toward moderation and reform. The French, in particular, believed that the

Ba'ath Party was still capable of liberal reform which, in any case, would be better and safer than the radical US prognosis of forcible "regime change."

Even the embattled Iraqi opposition was divided over this issue. The inability to agree on any form of common action had been the Achilles heel of the Iraqi opposition throughout its long struggle against Saddam's dictatorship. It would later prove far more costly after his overthrow. The two Kurdish parties, despite their concerns over past American betrayals, enthusiastically supported the call to war and even declared their readiness to participate in the coming campaign to topple Saddam. They showed a true willingness to unify their ranks prior to the coming war by quickly settling the main differences between the KDP and PUK and by convening a unified Kurdish parliament in 2002. The US also paraded a number of "dissidents," most of whom were either unknown in Iraq or had very dubious records. Such was the case with men like Ahmad Chalabi who had left Iraq as a child and was wanted in Jordan on charges of financial fraud. Ayad Allawi was known to some in Iraq for his past as a prominent Ba'athist official who left the country only because he had ended up on the wrong side of the numerous power struggles of the 1970s. Other than actively participating in the Ba'ath's worst crimes, his credibility in Iraq was questioned because of his admitted connections with American and British intelligence agencies. Both Chalabi and Allawi had been in the pay of the US government since the early 1990s through a special fund created under the Iraq Liberation Act. Perhaps most ironic of all, though, was the position taken by the Supreme Council for the Islamic Revolution in Iraq (SCIRI). As already noted in Chapter 2, SCIRI was a coalition of Shi'i Islamic groups supported by Iran. Their Badr Brigades, trained and supplied by Iran's Revolutionary Guards, were particularly close to the Islamic Republic's leaders. The obvious ideological contradictions notwithstanding, SCIRI's charismatic leader Ayatollah Muhammad Baqir al-Hakim strongly endorsed the American plan and gladly attended a conference of the Iraqi opposition organized and controlled by the US. The only prominent absentees from this meeting, held just prior to the war, were the Da'wa Party and the Communist Party. Both objected to the "hegemonic" American presence and to the whole case of an American-led war to topple the regime.

Within Iraq there were feelings of fear, confusion, and some hope that the dictatorship might soon be overthrown and the sanctions lifted. Such hopes were mixed with deep reservations about American intentions. Few had forgotten America's past support for Saddam during the 1980s, its betrayal of the March 1991 uprising, and its callous disregard for the suffering of the Iraqi people during the sanctions. All this in addition to the US's already tarnished image in the Middle East as a whole made for a very uncomfortable situation. Saddam, on the other hand, responded in the only way he knew how. In October 2002, he held another referendum on his presidency, and this time he received the *bay'a* of 100 percent of the electorate, prompting Iraqis to joke that Saddam was now even more popular than God himself. On the same day, and in celebration of this massive, albeit fabricated, popular show of confidence in his leadership, he pardoned most of the country's criminals and emptied Iraq's many jails. In one day, tens of thousands of hard-core criminals, including those convicted of murder, rape, burglary and highway robbery, spilled out into the streets of a country which would soon be at their mercy. Few, however, of the many political prisoners were included in this presidential pardon.

Invasion

Ignoring the United Nations and the various pleas from many allies and friends, the United States and Britain launched a full-scale war aimed at the overthrow of Saddam Hussein and the occupation of Iraq. The operation, codenamed "Iraqi Freedom," started on March 20, 2003, with a massive campaign of aerial bombardment followed closely by a ground assault. The whole operation tended to resemble a modern form of the German *blitzkrieg*, designed to inflict maximum damage on the enemy rather than to win over the hearts and minds of the population. If anything, the invasion was notable for the unexpected ease with which it unfolded. Despite small pockets of resistance here and there, the Iraqi army generally avoided direct confrontation and eventually melted away with the soldiers simply abandoning their posts and going home. There were some exceptions: near Baghdad's airport, for example, where an Iraqi counteroffensive was completely destroyed. When I visited the area a year later, scores of Iraqi tanks and armored vehicles littered both sides of the highway, their ammunition and engines gutted by looters. Within three weeks, American tanks entered Baghdad and the regime rapidly collapsed, most of its leaders, including Saddam, going into hiding. As with the 1991 war, no one knows the number of Iraqi casualties, though estimates run into tens of thousands killed. Only 128 American and 31 British soldiers died. The battle for Baghdad never took place, and even Saddam Hussein's own region around Tikrit surrendered without a fight. Essentially, the people of Iraq remained neutral in this war. Few were willing to risk their lives to protect a regime which had brought nothing but destruction and misery to the vast majority of the population. At the same time, however, no one received American troops "with flowers and candy" as some dissidents had promised. On 21 April, the US president confidently announced "mission accomplished" in Iraq, and by 1 May all combat operations had ended.

Simple, efficient, and deadly it might have been, but the American conquest of Iraq was a shambles in terms of postwar planning. The only important sites secured early in the war and put under military guard were the country's oil facilities, the Ministry of Oil and the Ministry of Interior. No humanitarian relief efforts followed the army, and few troops were left behind the main advance columns to secure the fallen towns and cities. Squabbles between the different US departments and agencies would have seemed comical if not for their tragic consequences. Questions which should have been settled long before the commencement of military operations were never clarified:

> Should the Pentagon be in charge of humanitarian aid, civil recon-struction, and state-building, tasks not favored by military admin-istrators? Who should be allowed to join the effort to rebuild Iraq? Is administrative experience and knowledge of Iraq and the region less important than political correctness? What are the risks and opportunities for American interests, and is there a danger these could conflict with Iraqi needs and interests? Who can we trust – do

we need to rely only on Iraqis from the diaspora and how will we know who can be rehabilitated inside Iraq?[5]

The lack of vision for the postwar management of the country was so acute that ensuing problems were inevitable.

Looting

It didn't take long for the first major setback to develop. Even before the fighting had subsided, residents from Baghdad's poorer neighborhoods, driven by hunger, greed, revenge, or curiosity, began to break in to government buildings. Many state employees had failed to receive their salaries for several months prior to the invasion, and there were rumors, some well founded, that government officials had stocked up scarce food in a number of buildings. Soldiers had brought home their weapons and a large number of criminals had been previously released by Saddam.[6] All institutions of state repression, including the ordinary police, had disappeared and not a single building was left guarded. American troops at the time did not number much more than 150,000 spread out over the entire country. This was woefully inadequate for a country roughly the size of California with a population of over 26 million desperate people. No curfew was declared nor were there any attempts to collect weapons. Even limited protection was denied as US commanders gave strict orders prohibiting any involvement in maintaining law and order. Cautious and still wary at first, the numbers grew with time as people broke in to government buildings suspected of containing food or money. Some broke in to the local or regional buildings of the dreaded security services just to see what these mysterious centers of terror really had inside them. Within about two or three days, the crowds had become aware of the complete impunity of their actions with American soldiers often looking on from a distance. At this point the crowds grew and the looting spread to include ministries, homes of prominent Ba'athists, research centers, universities, libraries, banks, hospitals, various companies, and weapons depots. In what must surely be regarded as a monumental blunder, American troops had captured a huge arms depot not far from Baghdad containing around 380 tons of powerful explosives, and then simply abandoned it. When several days later they returned, the depot had been completely emptied by looters. Many of these explosives were later used in attacking the US occupation forces and the new Iraqi government forces.

Within a short period the looting became organized under the control of criminal gangs. No one knows who these gang members were but it is not too hard to surmise that in addition to the criminals released by Saddam and soldiers looking for food and money, many were probably elements from the fallen regime's own security services who had become accustomed to criminal activities during the sanctions period. Looters took absolutely everything from computers, electronics, and heavy machinery, to furniture, fire extinguishers, books and light fixtures. Ministerial records and statistics were burned, hampering subsequent reconstruction efforts. Electricity cables throughout the country were stripped for their copper. Bronze statues were hauled away and later melted down for their metal as were guard rails and even sewer covers. Some gangs began to make incursions into residential neighborhoods, ordering terrified owners to dispense with all their possessions in broad daylight. But the most horrific crime was the looting of Iraq's National Museum, regarded as one of the finest in the world. An estimated 50,000 artefacts, many dating back to the earliest civilizations, were lost, though some were later found and returned. Looters used chainsaws to break into display booths, ruining many a priceless artefact in the process. Most of the buyers were foreigners with some even found among the US soldiers. A similar, arguably more sinister, attack occurred at the National Library. Here, after making away with some goods, the looters set fire to the building containing records and manuscripts of Iraq's past. Prior to the invasion, American forces were alerted to these and other important buildings and warned of the possibility of theft after the fall of the government. The warnings were simply ignored.

The looting went on for several weeks and though it subsided it never fully stopped. At the time of writing, the country remained at the mercy of looters and thieves who would strike at any hour with relative impunity. The one area that remained relatively free of such a breakdown was the north as Kurdish fighters proved capable of controlling the situation. Some market areas and neighborhoods, especially the poor Shiʻi slums, organized their own self-defense units, but overall the situation remains unsafe.

Other than emphasizing the sense of insecurity that had been regularly rising during the last ten years of Saddam's rule, the looting came as a shock to those who had hoped that the American occupation might bring an end to the country's deterioration. Only a few days after the end of Saddam's rule, most people were already infuriated at the inability of the occupation forces to provide basic law and order. The whole affair was so baffling that many came to believe it was intentionally encouraged by the Americans to destroy what remained of the country. The looting also added to the material destruction and set the process of reconstruction back many months. More importantly, it represented a massive blow to any sense of confidence in the new era under American tutelage. This, in turn, emboldened the malcontents and encouraged the embryonic resistance movement.

Resistance

Much to the surprise of the Americans and their Iraqi allies, resistance to the occupation started almost immediately after the fall of the regime. The resistance was, and continues to be, extremely complicated with a large number of groups with widely divergent aims. The looting had alerted some groups to the chaotic atmosphere and the inability of the occupation forces to control the situation. For most, the resistance actually started rather peacefully with demonstrations calling for jobs, salaries and the resumption of basic services. This is what happened, for example, in the city of Falluja soon after the invasion where demonstrations turned unruly and US troops fired on a crowd killing sixteen people. Falluja, like most towns, has a strong tribal ethos. To preserve a family's honor, its sons must carry out a vendetta against those who have harmed it even it is the American army. During 2003, acts of resistance appeared in both Sunni and Shiʻi areas but this began to change with the new administration's policies. The Coalition Provisional Authority (CPA), as the occupation government was called, enacted two orders that heightened the fears of major sections of the population. In May,

CPA head Paul Bremer abolished both the army and the Ba'ath Party. In one stroke, 350,000 soldiers were told they no longer had a salary or pension. Bremer's predecessor, J. Garner, who lasted only a few weeks, had planned to transform the army into a sort of labor corps, fixing the damaged infrastructure for extra pay. Bremer's decision was sudden, unplanned, and extremely dangerous, given the fact that almost all these soldiers still had possession of their weapons. But it does point to a tendency of almost unbelievable arrogance on behalf of Bremer's administration. The second order abolishing the Ba'ath Party held that all persons

> holding positions in the top three layers of management in every national government ministry, affiliated corporations and other government institutions (e.g. universities and hospitals) shall be interviewed for possible affiliation with the Ba'ath Party. [...] Any such persons determined to be full members [...] shall be removed from their employment. This includes those holding the more junior ranks of 'Udhu (Member) and 'Udhu 'Amil (Active Member), as well as those determined to be Senior Party Members.[7]

The de-Ba'athification Commission set to work eliminating the jobs of 30,000 to 50,000 people. In one fell swoop, the country, having already been deprived of its police and army, was now also deprived of its managerial class. There is little doubt that many top Ba'athists had blood on their hands and could no longer hold on to their posts even without the de-Ba'athification order. But the majority of Ba'athists, especially those occupying the lower levels, had been required to join as a condition of employment. The Commission was placed under the supervision of Ahmad Chalabi who quickly developed a reputation for corruption and nepotism. He used this powerful post to reward his supporters and punish his personal enemies. As most of the senior Ba'athists were Sunni Arabs, and many of the exiled groups now returning had a strong Shi'i bent, fears developed that the de-Ba'athification campaign might turn into a Sunni witchhunt.

Other factors encouraged men to join the gradually rising armed resistance. Many were driven by nationalist feelings and concerns that the Americans had come to permanently occupy the country. The visible construction of at least fourteen huge military bases failed to calm such fears. Some, from Saddam's numerous well-organized security services, simply reacted against the emergence of a new Iraq which despised them and sought to punish them for past crimes. The sentiments of one ex-member of the security apparatus are typical: "Was serving the country some sort of crime? [...] We were on top of the system. We had dreams [...] Now we are the losers. We lost our positions, our status, the [economic] security of our families, stability. Curse the Americans. Curse on them."[8]

American actions tended to amplify such feelings. Early on, American troops responded to attacks with heavy reprisals bordering on collective punishment, often resulting in the death of innocents. In 2004, for example, after Falluja had become a center of armed resistance, the Americans encircled the city and prevented all men aged fifteen to twenty from leaving. The 150,000 who did leave were put in camps suffering from poor conditions. That same year the city of Tal A'far, with a population of 300,000, was also besieged and had its water cut off for three days. In one aerial bombing of a village in 2003, a sheikh of the Dulaym tribe, who was actually friendly to the US, died prompting his sons to call for vengeance. Ignorance of the language and customs led to misunderstandings and conflicts. In both the Sunni Triangle and the Shi'i south, tribal customs predominate. For example, the use of dogs, considered ritually polluted, in house searches was regarded as a major offense, as was the bodily search of women. What made some of these cases worse was the Americans' increasing reliance on "private military firms" or, as Iraqis correctly call them, mercenaries. These troops, many employed by the Haliburton corporation, often ignored international conventions nor were they necessarily even US citizens. Most were appointed to guard individuals or institutions but some were used in field combat operations and in the interrogation of prisoners. The greatest symbol of American injustice, however, was the reopening of the Abu Ghraib prison compound. This large center was one of Saddam Hussein's despised symbols of repression. With the insurgency growing, the Americans began to make use of the prison to keep and interrogate suspects. After months of repeated warnings by the Red Cross and other agencies that conditions at Abu Ghraib represented a violation of the Geneva conventions, a scandal broke out that completely destroyed any chance of building trust. In 2004, newspapers began publishing a number of photographs leaked out from American soldiers at Abu Ghraib showing disturbing scenes of physical and psychological torture. Naked prisoners made to perform sexual acts with one another, dogs being set on defenseless captives, hooded men with electrical cables attached to their arms, legs, and genitals, and, perhaps most humiliating of all from the Iraqi perspective, a woman soldier holding a prisoner by a dog-leash and making him crawl on all fours. These and numerous other pictures, almost all showing American soldiers laughing, were widely published in the Iraqi press. The perception in the country was that the top US officials and commanders directly responsible for this act escaped prosecution. More importantly, few Iraqis were now willing to trust American claims of protecting human rights or supporting the development of democratic institutions.

As the anger increased, so did the frequency, effectiveness, and ruthlessness of the attacks. In August 2003, the United Nations building was devastated by a blast that killed UN Mission head Sergio de Mello, a man widely considered sympathetic to Iraqi concerns. Other attacks targeted economic centers, including the oil pipelines, and there were almost daily reports of American deaths. Spain decided to withdraw its forces after Madrid was subjected to a terrorist attack in April 2004, and the small reconstituted Iraqi army showed hesitation in fighting against fellow-Iraqis. According to some estimates, as of June 2006, there are currently around fifty groups leading the armed insurgency with between 20,000 and 50,000 fighters, about 10 percent of whom are not Iraqis, and many more active supporters. The most violent and least prone to compromises are the radical Wahhabi Islamic groups of the al-Qa'ida type. The Wahhabis are followers of an eighteenth-century reformer from central Arabia who called for a return to the pristine Islam evident at the time of the Prophet and his immediate successors. They regard secular regimes, including that of Saddam Hussein, as unacceptable, and all sects that deviate from their narrowly defined puritanical code as heresies that must be combated by force. In this regard, they do not necessarily differentiate between the Americans, whom they consider modern-day Christian crusaders, and the Shi'is. The latter, more than others, have come under vicious attacks targeting innocent civilians in a most indiscriminate manner. An example of one such Islamist leader was 'Umar Hussein Hadid of Falluja. He made his name during the last years of Saddam's rule by blowing up Falluja's only cinema theater. After the fall of the regime he organized locally against the looters and eventually turned his guns toward the Americans by joining Abu Mus'ab al-Zarqawi's al-Qa'ida branch. In 2004, he established a local Islamic governing council for Falluja that became notorious for public flogging and the beheading of supposed criminals. After the Americans captured Falluja in November 2004, Hadid fled and disappeared among the shadowy resistance groups.

Reconstruction and corporate looting

Soon after his arrival as head of the CPA, Paul Bremer declared: "We are not here as a colonial power. [...] We are here to turn over [authority] to the Iraqi people as soon as possible."[9] For the majority of Iraqis, these words were disturbingly similar to those of General Maude nearly a century earlier. The British went on to dominate Iraq for four decades before a violent revolution overthrew the monarchy. Bremer's deeds, especially in terms of restructuring the Iraqi economy, seemed to confirm this deep-seated fear of Western imperialism. For one thing, most of the CPA officials had little experience in actual economic reconstruction or nation-building efforts. Priority in appointments appeared focused on counterterrorism and counterinsurgency. Bremer himself, for example, was a retired foreign service official and a former head of the State Department's National Commission on Terrorism. Likewise, Andrew Erdman, the CPA's man in charge of reforming Iraqi higher education, was part of the Secretary of State's staff responsible for counterterrorism, homeland security, and Central Asian policy. He had no knowledge of Arabic, no prior training in university management and no experience in the Middle East. In fact, of all the numerous people who worked for the CPA between May 2003 and June 2004, only one senior official had any proficiency in Arabic. This "war on terror" mentality affected the CPA's whole conception of the reconstruction including the role of non-governmental organizations (NGOs). As Secretary of State Colin Powell stated: "Just as surely as our diplomats and military, American NGOs are out there serving and sacrificing on the front lines of freedom. NGOs are such a force multiplier for us, such an important part of our combat team."[10]

The goal of reconstruction was not even considered in any meaningful fashion until February 2003, just one month prior to the invasion. When planners finally did come together, they simply utilized a predetermined plan without considering the special needs and circumstances of the country. The plan included the complete overhaul of the economy to create a free market "capitalist's dream" within only a couple of months. In the words of Naomi Klein, Bush's plan "put simply, [...] was to lay out as much honey as possible, then sit back and wait for the flies."[11] The assumption, entirely false, was that Iraq resembled any other country with a "command economy" typical of the East European models. Liberalization of the laws and privatization of state enterprises were believed to be the necessary "shock therapy" leading to rapid growth. Very little attention went into long-term planning, as "market forces" were expected to kick into place and direct the economy into the future. More problematic, especially for future American–Iraqi trust, was the assumption that Iraqis were a backward people who had little to offer the reconstruction project. A good example of this stereotyping can be seen in the comments of Joanne Dickow, the CPA's representative on women's issues. Commenting on a meeting she had had with select women's representatives she said: "There was this incredible sense by the Iraqi women of 'Oh my goodness, what do you mean we're going to get involved in politics?' And there was this sense of 'Oh, these are doctors, lawyers and engineers.' [...] Getting them to understand that this was their time was probably the hardest job of all at the beginning."[12] It's not clear exactly which women she was referring to but one wonders whether CPA officials ever bothered to acquaint themselves with Iraqi history. As recently as 1993, UNICEF observed that "rarely do women in the Arab world enjoy as much power and support as they do in Iraq."[13] Going further back, Iraq could boast a number of women leaders both in government and the opposition including the Arab world's first woman minister. Currently, a number of women, including many who refused to deal with the CPA, hold prominent positions in several parties and lead various local NGOs.

In September 2003, Bremer issued the controversial Order No. 39 authorizing "foreign investor[s] [...] to make foreign investments in Iraq on terms no less favorable than those applicable to an Iraqi investor" in all sectors except oil.[14] This represented a radical break with previous policy and a clear violation of international law which prevents occupying powers from changing the economic laws. Iraq's progressive tax system was also changed to a flat tax of 15 percent while tariffs and customs duties were virtually eliminated. Bremer later moved to encourage rapid privatization despite significant Iraqi opposition. This was assisted by the constant pressure imposed by Iraq's Western creditors organized in such institutions as the Paris Club. In November 2004, the Paris Club presented a list of conditions for Iraq to meet in return for writing off portions of its $120 billion debt. Foremost among these was the demand to privatize its state industries and cut subsidies.

The problem was that the economy and infrastructure were so devastated that, far from encouraging investments, such measures actually promoted massive capital flight and the importation of cheap goods. The result was that Iraq's local industries couldn't compete and unemployment remained extremely high. The collapse of state institutions also meant the disappearance of many services and the social safety-net which protected workers and small businesses. The whole notion of providing assistance was an anathema to the free market fundamentalists of the CPA. In the words of one official: "Our goal was to help Iraqis understand that government shouldn't squelch growth, and that there wasn't much it had to do to stimulate growth."[15] But Iraq was just emerging from decades of sanctions, wars, and a period of looting and lawlessness which left its economy badly in need of protective measures. No effort was made to provide credit or training, and Iraqi experts were pointedly not included in decision-making processes. This not only hampered development materially, it also added to the sense of anger at being excluded and alienated from the whole process. Refusal to consult with Iraqis, who knew the system well, or to consider subsidies in some areas, had wide-ranging implications. For example, aid to railway transportation was halted, resulting in a breakdown of service which affected the domestic transfer of fertilizers and cement. As a result, the country had to import both of these products despite having the ability to produce them locally. Agriculture received no assistance in terms of irrigation works or state-subsidized fertilizers. This led to more labor migrants flocking to the cities at a time when the country could ill-afford to handle them.

In October 2003, the US Congress approved the huge sum of $18.4 billion for the reconstruction of Iraq's economy. While this looks good on paper, as of this writing only a tiny fraction (some say as low as 3 percent) has actually been spent. Over 95 percent of the funds spent on contracts came from the country's oil revenues, frozen assets, and loans on future oil sales. Contracts covering the most important sectors were handed out by the CPA early on without open bidding or competition. US companies received the lion's share of the contracts, especially Haliburton, Bechtel, and Fluor. Initially, the Americans justified the exclusion of European, Russian, and Canadian firms on the ground that these countries had not supported the invasion. But even American companies were denied an equal playing field with firms that had good connections to the White House. Young companies, such as Blackwater USA, which were bordering on bankruptcy before the invasion, were transformed overnight into some of the world's most profitable firms. The chaotic and lawless climate in Iraq provided ideal conditions for shameless profiteering, corruption, and fraud. A clear example concerned the firm Custer Battles. By all accounts, this contractor overcharged the CPA by millions of dollars, double-billed for salaries, and created sham companies. The big shock, however, came when former employees failed in their attempts to sue the company for defrauding the American government. Essentially, the courts failed to recognize the CPA as an American entity. On the other hand, American firms in Iraq enjoy immunity from prosecution under Iraqi law. This means that firms such as Custer Battles were basically answerable to no one. In other cases, the stakes were much higher. Bechtel, for example, won a contract for the repair of the country's water infrastructure. According to the contract's wording, signed on April 17, 2003, Bechtel makes the pledge that "within 12 months potable water supply will be restored in all urban centers."[16] A year later a report concluded that "Bechtel, to this day, continues to get paid for work which it is simply not getting done."[17] At the time of this writing, water and sewage treatment remains well below prewar levels, especially in the major urban centers. What makes the matter particularly distressing is that problems associated with water contamination account for over half of hospital cases involving children. Rather than being held accountable for its failure to deliver its contract obligations, Bechtel was rewarded with additional contracts placing it in line to assume full private control of the country's water delivery systems. Such misuse of funds was so widespread, possibly affecting $9 billion, it prompted the anti-corruption group Transparency International to warn that Iraq's reconstruction program could very well have the dubious honor of becoming the biggest corruption scandal in history.

Most of the contracts relating to oil went to Haliburton or one of its subsidiaries. This still represents a potential bonanza not only because of the huge quantities available, but, more importantly, because Iraqi oil is probably the world's cheapest to extract. Some estimate that Iraqi oil costs as little as between 50 cents to one dollar per barrel to produce.[18] Much to the ire of Iraqis, the CPA sold Iraqi oil to the US and Britain at below world prices. The US government has great hopes that Iraqi oil can one day reduce America's dependence on Saudi Arabia. This, however, still requires massive investments to increase Iraqi production from its current 2 billion barrels a day to at least 8 billion barrels a day. Much of the work in oil and other sectors is being subcontracted to smaller firms. This has the effect of wasting millions of dollars but it did prove valuable in cases where Iraqi firms picked up the subcontracts. In the meantime, the country is forced to suffer from some truly odd practices concerning the sale and consumption of petroleum. In the south, for example, more fishermen now prefer to smuggle Iraqi oil purchased cheaply from the thriving black market. The oil is then smuggled to surrounding countries or as far away as India resulting in its scarcity domestically. In 2005, Iraq, one of the world's foremost oil producers, had to spend over $200 million per month on imported oil products.

A lot of the reconstruction problems are directly the result of the dire security situation. In 2004, an estimated $8 billion was lost to sabotage. Insurgents have used ruthless tactics of suicide bombers, kidnaping, and terrifying televised killings of foreign workers to drive investors away. Such tactics did have an impact as security concerns were the chief cause behind the cessation of many projects. Significantly, projects in which Iraqi firms are in charge demonstrated much more resilience. Instead of beefing up security, foreign contractors tended to withdraw into the heavily fortified presidential palace compound, now dubbed the "Green Zone." Isolated and cut off from field operations, many of the projects became even more prone to corruption and sabotage. Not all the attacks were politically motivated. The lack of electricity, for example, has encouraged the rise of a sort of lawless entrepreneurship with businessmen setting up small private generators selling electricity to local communities. With time, such businesses sprouted up everywhere creating a class whose interests are directly harmed by attempts to fix the power grid. In many ways the deficiencies of the reconstruction directly fed the insurrection and the insecurity added to the problems of reconstruction. The continuing lack of proper electric power was especially problematic. Summarizing local feelings one CPA official said: "The Iraqis would ask why the Americans could hit a tank hiding between two buildings from 3,000 feet away, but they couldn't turn on the electricity. And they assumed the reason had to be something sinister. [...] The rumor mill would be that the Americans are punishing us."[19]

Despite all the odds, some real accomplishments were achieved. The Iraqi dinar was pegged to the dollar and stabilized, adding much relief to the business community. Inflation was brought under control and the scarcity of food never materialized. Civil service salaries were increased and paid regularly with a corresponding rise in annual per capita incomes from an average of $400 to $1,400. Civil society is making a valiant attempt to emerge, with over 4,000 registered and 9,000 unregistered local NGOs. A good example of such an organization is the al-Amal Association with projects currently spanning the entire country. When I visited their healthcare projects around the impoverished Najaf countryside in 2004, I saw a locally organized and funded exhibition on nutrition, a mobile clinic, and a locally organized conference on the nature of NGO work. Three aspects of al-Amal's work were particularly telling. First, there is a real collective leadership which is non-sectarian and democratic. Here it appears that the absence of democracy under the Ba'ath did not prove to be an insurmountable obstacle. Second, despite their desperate need for assistance, they have steadfastly refused to accept American funding. Though this is certainly a very passive form of opposition, it might prove to be extremely important in the long run. Third, the high level of local grassroots participation, which is especially conspicuous in its non-sectarian culture, speaks volumes as to the progressive potential still present in the country. Whether such potential will eventually triumph is obviously not clear but neither is it a hopeless illusion. Most visible are the proliferation of newspapers, magazines, books of all sorts, radio stations, and more than twenty local television channels representing a broad array of opinions. The media in Iraq today are perhaps the freest in the Arab world but they are gradually being hemmed in by the rising sectarian parties. The region which has achieved the most in terms of reconstruction is the Kurdish north. Good security has allowed for a construction boom and relatively strong investments in every sector. White collar workers there now earn seven times their salaries prior to the invasion. Professionals and unskilled workers are being drawn to the north from other areas in the country, prompting local authorities to voice some concern about preserving the region's ethnically Kurdish identity.

Post-Saddam politics

From April 2003, when Saddam's regime fell to American forces, to June 2004, Iraq was administered directly by the American-dominated CPA. The CPA viewed the resistance as remnants of the Ba'athist state and thus took broad measures to destroy all vestiges of that state. This was roundly applauded by Kurdish and Shi'i groups, who continued to lobby for a weak central authority. Under pressure from Iraqi groups, Bremer agreed to the establishment of an advisory committee called the Iraqi Governing Council (IGC) composed of twenty-five individuals associated with various opposition groups. Membership of the IGC was partially determined by sectarian allocations, the first time this had been done in Iraq's modern history. During the sanctions, sectarianism was a latent force gradually coming into the open. This step encouraged its further development and set the tone for the subsequent rise of sectarian politics in the country. The Americans initially pushed Ahmad Chalabi to the fore, a relatively unknown figure in Iraq, but he later fell out of favor after he allegedly stole over $30 million from the US and passed sensitive secrets to the Iranians.

The majority of Iraq's new political parties had been in exile for many decades before returning in 2003. There they suffered from the influences of host countries, such as Iran and Syria, and from a sense of alienation which tended to promote excessive factionalism and sectarianism. In general, post-Saddam political movements can be grouped into four distinct categories. The first includes the Kurdish nationalist parties, of which the KDP and PUK are the largest. Though their relations were anything but smooth, the KDP, PUK, and other smaller parties, had successfully established a working relationship with one another. The Kurdish parliament continued to function, and the Kurdish parties normally presented a united front when dealing with outsiders. Kurdish politics was defined through a determination to protect their autonomy by insisting on a federal relationship with Baghdad. The main parties also emphasized a secular agenda and essentially enjoyed good relations with American forces. At the time when the rest of the country suffered from lawlessness, looting and armed insurrection, the Kurdish government proved capable of maintaining security and order. The only exception to this picture is the persistence of Islamist groups such as the previously-mentioned Islamist Movement of Kurdistan and the more radical Ansar al-Islam Movement. Both have gained support by criticizing the rampant corruption and nepotism of the two dominant parties and by receiving assistance from Iran. The latter clashed repeatedly with the Kurdish government and could become a source of instability in the future.

The second group comprises a variety of secular parties espousing a liberal agenda. It includes such old parties as the Iraqi Communist Party and the National Democratic Party. Others formed around important figures such as Adnan al-Pachachi, Ghazi al-Yawar, and

Ayad 'Allawi. The latter attracted a number of moderate Ba'athists who believe that there could still be room for them in the new order. The third group is composed of a number of Sunni Islamist parties who later formed the so-called Iraq Accord Front. Ideologically they are critical of secularism and seek the formation of an Islamic government. They are, however, deeply worried about Iranian influences and emphasize the country's Arab identity. Based primarily in the Sunni Triangle, they worry that a federal arrangement would leave their constituency impoverished since, unlike the Kurdish north and the Shi'i south, their territory contains very little oil. Sunni Arabs have been the most supportive of the anti-American insurrection though it is wrong to assume that they are automatically sympathetic to the Ba'ath. Groups like the Islamic Party of Iraq were suppressed by Saddam, and during the 1990s several anti-Ba'athist coup attempts originated from this region. There is, however, a fear that the de-Ba'athification campaign punished all Sunnis regardless of their affiliations. Ba'athists have therefore found it easier to form alliances with elements from this group. Lastly, the largest and most powerful group includes Shi'i parties and organizations. After the fall of the dictatorship, various Shi'i militias emerged and took control of the streets in almost all the southern cities and the slums of East Baghdad. We have already made reference to the SCIRI, Da'wa and Sadrists. Others include a Sadrist off-shoot known as the Fadhila Party and followers of Grand Ayatollah 'Ali Sistani. These and other smaller Shi'i groups came together to form the United Iraqi Alliance under the leadership of 'Abdul-'Aziz al-Hakim, the spiritual leader of SCIRI. The most important common denominator uniting this diverse and highly fractious group is the sense of past injustices done to the Shi'is and the demand for political power commensurate with their status as the majority of Iraqis. All of these groups suffer from deep fissures along various lines. The Sadr Movement, in particular, has generally ignored the American presence and sought to aggressively seize control of public institutions. The movement's leader, Muqtada al-Sadr, was roundly applauded by broad sections of Shi'is and Sunnis when he refused an invitation by the US administrator to participate in forming a government by declaring: "I don't want the chair of the government because it will be controlled by the

US and I don't want to be controlled by the US."[20] He even directly challenged the authority of the Grand Ayatollah Sistani, partly on the grounds that he is Iranian not Arab.

Between May 2003 and June 2004, the Iraqi Governing Council struggled to have an impact over the domineering CPA. Sistani criticized foreign rule and refused to meet with Bremer. As a result of the mounting pressure, punctuated with ever-rising acts of violence, Bremer agreed to hand over the reins of power to an interim government headed by the American-picked Ayad 'Allawi. Its primary function was to prepare for national elections but the American presence remained ubiquitous. 'Allawi's government had no control over the army or the finances, could not change any of the CPA's orders, and all ministries remained under American supervision. 'Allawi himself was deeply disliked as an old Ba'athist and his period in office confirmed a tendency toward a new authoritarianism with increasing detentions and curfews. The chaotic situation in the country seemed only to get worse with time and in a desperate bid to achieve some legitimacy, an announcement was made that elections would be held for a National Assembly. The whole affair served only to exacerbate tensions. Rather than focusing on a bottom-up approach with the steady development of civil society and local government, the plunge into national elections at a time of lawlessness brought the most demagogic elements to the fore. This was not an unforeseen development. In a report written prior to the invasion for the US-funded Future of Iraq Project, its Iraqi authors noted:

> The holding of local elections within a period of not more than 12 months from the fall of the regime has many advantages. It will create genuinely representative local administrative authorities whose presence will complement the role of the Transitional Authority. It will introduce politics at the grassroots level and provide a trial run for the national elections, which follow at the end of the transitional period. And it will help expand the nucleus of potential political leaders in Iraq to encompass senior civil servants, professionals and technocrats who are not tainted by their past.[21]

Most Sunni parties boycotted the national elections on the

grounds that the insurrection prevented their meaningful participation. In the end, 8.5 million people voted in the January 2005
elections in a courageous show of popular defiance. The general
atmosphere of insecurity, coupled with the gradual development of
sectarianism evident during the sanctions period, determined the
outcome. In the continued absence of state institutions, most people
voted for sectarian and ethnic parties which they felt had a better
chance of clamping down on lawlessness. Out of a total of 275 available seats, the Shiʻi and Kurdish lists won 215 (see Table 5.1). One of
the most surprising results, and an indication of the changed times,
was the poor showing of the once popular Communist Party which
gained only two seats. The formation of a Shiʻi–Kurdish government
heightened the fears of the Sunni community as they began to feel
even more marginalized.

The chief task before the Assembly was the writing of a draft
constitution which would then be presented for a national referendum. The whole constitution-writing process created more divisions
than consensus. For one thing, the American administration, facing
increasing criticism at home, demanded a quick, symbolic show of
progress. The media had little access to the secretive meetings, limiting the public's engagement. Important Sunni figures did not have
an input because they had boycotted the process. The main problem
revolved round the question of centralization. While the parties
agreed on a federal arrangement with Kurdistan, they remained
deeply divided over the powers of the central government. In the end
the document represented a hurried patchwork of poorly worded,

TABLE 5.1 Comparative results of Iraqi elections

Electoral list	Results in seats	
	January 2005	December 2005
United Iraqi Alliance (Shiʻi)	140	128
Kurdistan Coalition	75	53
Iraq Accord Front (Sunni)	-boycotted-	44
Iraqi National List (Secular)	40	25
Others	20	25
Total	275	275

sometimes contradictory, phrases with essential components left unfinished. To ensure Sunni participation, an eleventh-hour agreement was struck permitting the amendment of the constitution within a short period of its expected adoption. The referendum was held in October 2005, and yielded a 78.5 percent vote in favor of its adoption. Despite this high percentage, the vote in fact betrayed a profound lack of consensus as the Arab Sunni population overwhelmingly voted against the constitution. The constitution renders the central government almost powerless and fails to establish a coherent system of checks and balances. It encourages the formation of federal regions in the oil-rich areas while depriving the Sunni regions of economic security. On the other hand, the document did contain some progressive features not present in most constitutions of the Middle East. It stipulates, for example, that women make up least 25 percent of the Assembly's representatives, citizenship can be passed to the children from either the mother or father, and the president of the republic need not be a Muslim man.

A final election was held at the end of 2005 for the National Assembly and, again, the tendency toward deepening sectarianism continued with an even more dismal showing for the secular parties (Table 5.1). Even such small communities as the Christian Assyrians and the Turkomen preferred to field ethnically-defined lists and most clerics declared their support for their own religious parties. The victory of the Shi'i list, however, soon brought to the fore the latent tensions within the Alliance as the different parties failed to agree on a candidate for prime minister. By February 2006, the United Iraqi Alliance eventually agreed on Ibrahim al-Ja'fari, the leader of the Da'wa Party, but not before serious confrontations which may yet come back to haunt them. Ja'fari's nomination failed to win a majority of votes in Parliament, however, and after five months of devastating paralysis the contending parties finally agreed on Nuri al-Maliki (also from the Da'wa Party) as a compromise candidate. Al-Maliki's leadership has raised hopes that it can, despite the pronounced sectarianism of the groups involved, establish some form of national unity government.

An interesting feature of post-Saddam politics has been the rise of religious figures like the Grand Ayatollah 'Ali Sistani. Throughout the tumultuous ordeal, he was a force for moderation and calm, urging his followers to practice restraint in the face of overtly sectarian attacks. In September 2005, in response to repeated calls by al-Qaʻida's Abu Musʻab al-Zarqawi to wage war on the Shiʻis, he issued the following message: "The fundamental aim of these threats [...] is to sow sedition [...] and ignite the flames of civil war. [...] We call on the believers [...] to continue to exercise restraint accompanied by increased caution [... and] to strive toward what strengthens the nation's unity and amity among its sons and daughters."[22]

Sistani has remained hesitant about playing an openly political role as he hails from the quietist branch of Shiʻi Islam. He has made repeated calls to religious leaders urging them to avoid seeking political positions, though he did implicitly endorse the Shiʻi list. His considerable stature notwithstanding, repeated attacks against innocent Shiʻis and their shrines have made it far more difficult to rein in his followers. This was especially evident in February 2006, after the bombing of the ʻAskariya mausoleum in Samarra, one of the most sacred Shiʻi shrines in the world. In this climate, the feeble nature of the state contributed directly to rising dependence on primary associations. "I hope the criminals will receive the death penalty," said a father who had just lost a loved one after one such attack. "If not, I plan to resolve the matter by my tribe. I will have my tribe kill members of theirs if the government doesn't do anything."[23] Slowly, these attacks have led to the marginalization of secular groups as well as voices of moderation like that of Sistani. In their stead, groups such as that of Muqtada al-Sadr, the son of Sadr II mentioned in Chapter 4, with their fiery defiance of US authority and a readiness to use violence to protect their interests, have gained much support. The Sadrists have also drawn some support from Sunni groups for their insistence on the Arab identity of Iraq and their expressions of solidarity with the Sunnis of Falluja in the face of US attacks. In the climate of chaos and sectarian clashes approaching full-scale civil war, the niceties of democracy and rule of law have gradually faded. Today the Ministry of Interior is gaining the same reputation for unlawful detention and torture it once held under Saddam.

Regional involvement

The original intention of the American invasion, publicly anyway, was to overthrow tyranny in Iraq and send a clear warning to other "rogue" states in the region, especially Iran and Syria. Instead, it has driven these states toward greater cooperation with one another and with other anti-American groups such as Hizbullah of Lebanon, Hamas of the Palestinian Territories, and the Sadrist Movement in Iraq. It also encouraged Iran to multiply its efforts in developing its nuclear program. The chaotic situation in Iraq has aided the rise of such violent groups as al-Qa'ida and created the foundation for the emergence of proxies who are more than willing to strike at US soldiers. These groups have received a boost from the overwhelming perception in the region of the US as an aggressive imperialist power. Regional tensions have, in turn, played a destructive role in Iraq as competing parties, desperate for any kind of assistance, are willing to give much in return to potential sponsors. Regional involvement could prove to be the most important factor determining whether or not a civil war will erupt in Iraq.

Up to now, neither the US or Britain, nor any of the surrounding countries wish to see an open civil war leading to the dismemberment of Iraq. Such a scenario would surely affect these countries' own heterogeneous populations, perhaps encouraging them to demand adjustments to their status. In September 2005, Saudi Arabia's foreign minister expressed his country's concern when addressing an American audience:

> If you allow for this – for a civil war to happen between the Shi'ites and the Sunnis, Iraq is finished forever. It will be dismembered. It will [...] cause so many conflicts in the region that it will bring the whole region into turmoil. [...] The Iranians would enter the conflict because of the south, the Turks because of the Kurds, and the Arabs ... will definitely be dragged into the conflict.[24]

Of all the countries involved in Iraq, Iran is clearly the most influential. There is a profound irony in the fact that the American invasion achieved for Iranian leaders their wish to see Islamist Shi'i parties ruling in Iraq. Iran has used its historic ties with SCIRI and the Da'wa Party to extend its reach into the country. It also sent its own agents directly along with the hundreds of thousands of pilgrims now entering Iraq to visit Shiʻi shrines long denied them under Saddam. Iranian influence was driven home in early 2006 when both the Badr Brigades and the Sadrists declared their willingness to turn their guns against the Americans in Iraq should the US attack Iran over its nuclear program. This influence raised alarms in the Arab Gulf countries who fear both Iranian expansionism and the "awakening" of their own Shiʻi communities. Shiʻis comprise 11 percent of Saudi Arabia's population, located mainly in its oil-rich eastern provinces, 25 percent of Kuwaitis and 70 percent of Bahrainis. In December 2004, King Abdullah of Jordan warned that Iran was seeking to establish a "Shiʻi Crescent" with Iraq, Syria, and Lebanon. The reaction to these fears has been two-fold. First, the Arab League successfully convened a reconciliation conference in Cairo in November 2005, which brought together all the contending parties. It was a first step but it did help avert a major crisis at the time. Future meetings are planned to take place in Iraq. The second response has been more ominous with Arab countries increasing their aid to Sunni groups in the hope of checking Shiʻi power. This has deepened the divisions rather than helped heal the wounds.

National reconciliation or sectarian civil war?

In a report prepared for the International Crisis Group, the authors observed that "2005 will be remembered as the year Iraq's latent sectarianism took wings, permeating the political discourse and precipitating incidents of appalling violence and sectarian 'cleansing.'"[25] Prior to the American invasion, social sectarianism was still benign, with mixed marriages quite common and mixed neighborhoods the rule in most urban areas. Saddam's rule, while favoring Sunni Arabs for high posts, was equally repressive toward Sunnis when faced with acts of insubordination. The suppression of civil society, followed by the tribal pecking order created during the sanctions period, and finally the decapitation of the state by the American occupation, encouraged the overt development of sectarianism. Iraq's urban middle classes, which suffered the most during the sanctions, had the reputation of being staunchly secular. In some ways, the rise of sectarianism can be directly linked with the suppression of civil society and the decline of the middle classes. The CPA's policies pushed the contending parties further into the sectarian quagmire. For one thing, the CPA simply did not have sufficient troops to police a country which was now deprived of its own security institutions. Ideologically, American strategists had a simplistic notion of Iraq being divided into three more or less homogeneous communities, Kurds, Sunnis, and Shi'is, with the Sunnis representing the foundation of the Ba'athist state. The early policies of the CPA were geared toward empowering Kurdish and Shi'i representatives at the expense of Sunnis. This reductionist view determined the decisions leading up to the disbandment of the army, the de-Ba'athification campaign, and the distribution of seats in the Iraqi Governing Council according to a quota system. As early as May 2003, the American military governor of Mosul helped set up a city council using a system of proportional representation along sectarian lines. A similar system was used for other cities like Kirkuk and also for the appointment to ministries. The insurgency confirmed early anti-Sunni bias in American thinking, and the response has been heavy-handed, affecting whole communities. In the end, the Sunnis felt that they were being singled out for punishment, reinforcing a defensive sectarian identity. In point of fact, such hard-core Sunni areas as Tikrit, Samarra, and Mosul, did not offer any resistance during the invasion and as of the time of writing remain relatively free of sustained insurgent operations.

In the meantime, some Wahhabi groups like al-Qa'ida developed a brutal strategy of actively stoking sectarian feelings by attacking Shi'is, specifically in the hopes of inviting an anti-Sunni backlash. Zarqawi, the then leader of al-Qa'ida in Iraq, felt that the climate of chaos and sectarianism improved his chances of recruiting for a religious war. In a letter distributed in September 2005, he condemned Shi'ism as "a religion that does not meet with Islam [...] [whose followers] were throughout history a twig in the throats of the people of Islam, a dagger that strikes them in the back, the cavity that destroys the structure, and the bridge over which the enemies of Islam pass."[26] In March 2004, in the first major attack on Shi'is, 100 worshipers were killed in separate suicide bombings in Baghdad and Karbala. This writer, present at the time of the bombing in Baghdad, was struck by the manner in which Sunnis rallied to condemn the attack and donate blood for the victims. Such acts of solidarity were repeated on numerous occasions and the media tried their best to highlight them, but the repetition and ruthlessness of the attacks, which often targeted the most innocent and vulnerable, eventually had an impact. This was especially evident after the previously-mentioned bombing of the 'Askariya shrine in February 2006.

The elections brought Shi'i parties to power with a strong public mandate to address the security problem. These parties were ill-equipped to develop a mature, patient solution as they remained shackled by parochialism and lacking a broad national vision. Having been trained and supplied by Iran, groups like the SCIRI used the Ministry of Interior and sections of the new army to settle old scores and respond to the sectarian attacks in a like-minded manner. Once in control of the government, SCIRI, the Da'wa and the Sadrists hurried to build up a network of patronage based on sectarian ties. The most important figure in this tit-for-tat approach to the violence has been the Minister of Interior Bayan Jabr Sawlagh. Sawlagh was the head of SCIRI's militia, the Badr Brigades, which were established in Iran in 1982. The Badr Brigades recruited initially from the Iraqi POWs during the Iran–Iraq War and depended on heavy religious indoctrination. Under Sawlagh, the police and the Interior Ministry's crack commando units were restructured along purely sectarian lines, animated by a strong desire for vengeance against perceived wrongs done to the Shi'is as a whole. In November 2005, secret "death squads" and torture chambers run by the Interior Ministry were uncovered. Lately, an extremely disturbing development has been the eviction of families in a process of "sectarian cleansing." If this process continues, it makes civil war more likely as the last ties bridging the communities are severed. Checkpoints have been set up by rival militias around Baghdad with instructions to detain, and often kill, people based on their religious affiliation.

This separation is also evident in the nascent state institutions. For example, the so-called Wolf Brigade is now divided into Sunni and Shi'i sections with each used to target the opposing community. Ministries have become the personal fiefdoms of political parties which staff them with supporters, usually along sectarian lines. Even the new professional army, which the Americans have made the main focus for the construction of a new Iraq, shows signs of being divided along Sunni, Shi'i, and Kurdish lines. Ironically, Kurdish leaders who have long fought for autonomy and greater separation, are today doing more to keep the country unified than any of the Arab leaders. There is a greater awareness in Kurdistan that the dismemberment of the country will surely result in Turkish and Iranian intervention, leading to the loss of even limited regional sovereignty. The most hopeful signs, however, have only just occurred: the Iraqi parliament has agreed on a government of national unity with representatives from all the major political blocs and a program of amnesty and national reconciliation. While, at the time of writing, it remains too soon to reflect on its performance, there is now renewed hope that a political agreement on the level of the leadership might lead to the lowering of tensions at the local level. More importantly, the agreement inaugurated a political process which, while still full of flaws, is at least nationally inclusive. Should it survive for what will surely be a very difficult first year, the country might yet pull itself out of its present morass.

Epilogue

Samuel Noah Kramer, that unrivaled historian of ancient Iraq, once reflected on what caused this land to become the birthplace of human civilization:

> What turned Mesopotamia into a fruitful paradise and made it a creative force was the intellectual endowment and psychological make-up of its people. Observant, reflective and pragmatic, they tended to grasp what was fundamental and exploit what was possible. Unlike virtually all other ancient peoples, the Mesopotamians evolved a way of life guided by a sense of moderation and balance. Materially and spiritually – in religion and ethics, in politics and economics – they struck a viable mean between reason and fancy, freedom and authority, the knowable and the mysterious.[1]

In considering the recent history of Iraq and the condition it currently finds itself in, one cannot help but wonder at how remote and alien modern Iraqis are from their illustrious ancestors. In practically every meaningful way, Iraqi society today is the very opposite of moderation. Violence and social fragmentation underscore a new level of extremism which now threatens the very survival of Iraq as a unified state. A sure sign of the decay in Iraqi politics is that up to the mid-1970s social movements were still expressed in terms of ideological parties, trade unions, and women's and students' associations, that cut horizontally across religious and ethnic ties. For sure, sectarian, ethnic, or tribal feelings did affect the smooth functioning of these institutions but at least the country was moving in the direction of greater national integration. Now, almost uniformly, politics is dominated by an openly sectarian or ethnic ethos. The cause lies in the four decades of relentless hammering of social institutions, starting with Ba'athist repression, wars, sanctions, and continuing with the American occupation. Today, out of a total population of 25 million, there are about 1.5 million permanently disabled, 600,000 disappeared, and 5 million refugees, 1.5 million of them internally. The country is littered with 30 million landmines, the highest concentration in the world. Since the American occupation, between 35,000 and 50,000 people have died. Last year there were 5,000 cases of kidnaping and, currently, an average of between fifty to sixty people die every day in what many are already calling the early signs of civil war. Three years after the fall of Saddam's dictatorship, the new political elite has demonstrated its inability to rise above sectarian divisions, local militias are beginning effectively to rule the country, and ethnic and religious cleansing are increasing. Under such conditions, elections and constitutional referendums have actually fanned sectarian flames rather than acted as the basis for a new, more unified, country.

In the midst of this, America's 135,000 troops face an impossible situation. Their presence has thus far kept the antagonists apart, but the US's image as an imperialist occupier has also heightened tensions. America's conflict with Iran has likewise added to the complexity of the situation as this battle is being partially played out on Iraqi soil with devastating results. If these trends continue the country will surely fall victim to full-fledged sectarian strife. Should a Sunni–Shiʻi civil war erupt, the casualties and destruction of the recent past will pale in comparison. The country's largest cities of Baghdad, Mosul, Kirkuk, and Basra are all religiously and ethnically mixed, as are many neighborhoods, tribes, and even individual families. Aside from the inherent difficulty of separating the communities, rump states are bound to do everything in their power to grab oil-rich land and surrounding countries will be drawn in to protect their interests. The crisis facing the state of Iraq should not be seen as an indictment of its "invention" by the British in 1920, but rather as an example of the perils facing any country which has crushed its civil society. Indeed, the amazing fact about Iraq today is that even after enduring terrible hardships, it is still stubbornly clinging on to its unity. Nor are the problems simply the result of American ineptitude, but rather are an awkward, unfocused rejection by a myriad of groups including Saddam loyalists, of an imperialistic attempt to transform the Iraqi economy to suit the neo-conservatives' notions of US interests.

One hopeful sign is that none of the Iraqi groups or surrounding countries wants to see a civil war. All the parties involved, the Kurds included, are convinced that a civil war leading to the dismemberment of the country cannot be contained and will surely bring ruin to everyone within Iraq and the region as a whole. Perhaps now that the country is looking squarely at the abyss, reason will prevail and compromises will be struck. There is a pressing need to form, and maintain for as long as possible, a government of national unity representing all the major political groups regardless of the number of parliamentary seats they may currently occupy. Efforts must be made to increase international peacekeepers at the expense of American troops as a first step to ending the occupation. Foreign contracts need to be renegotiated in a more transparent manner with a view to ending American's present monopoly over the economy. Oil, the foundation of the economy for decades to come, must remain firmly under the control of the central state with guarantees for equitable distribution among the country's regions. The country has already reached a consensus on the establishment of a federal region in Kurdistan because of its unique history and national makeup. Discussions about the establishment of other federal regions should be delayed for several years until the country can emerge from its present dangers. There are currently signs that the sectarian coalitions themselves are beginning to break up because of other competing identities. Still, the concept of administrative decentralization to the provincial level is important to guard against future dictatorships. Whatever amendments are made to the existing constitution, the parties must make a strong commitment to the development and strengthening of institutions of civil society as the foundation of democracy and national unity. Above all, however, the country has a desperate need to recapture that sense of moderation and balance which was the hallmark of the cradle of civilization.

Notes

Introduction

1 A large number of works take this approach but among the most recent are Dodge, *Inventing Iraq* (2003); and Catherwood, *Churchill's Folly* (2004).

2 Catherwood, *Churchill's Folly*, p. 16.

3 Ibid., p. 14.

1 The rise of the modern state

1 The exact year of the decisive battle, known as the Battle of Qadisiyya, is not known; most historians favor either 636 or 637 and a few argue for 638.

2 The most important treaties were those of Amasya in 1555, Zuhab (also known as the Treaty of Qasr-i Shirin) in 1639, and Erzerum in 1847.

3 Quoted in Nakash, *The Shi'is of Iraq*, p. 70. The Hanafi and Shafi'i schools are branches of Sunni Islam whereas the Ja'fari and Zaydi are of Shi'i Islam. The shari'a is the Islamic law or code of behavior based on the Qur'an and the teachings of the Prophet Muhammad.

4 Shields, "Mosul Questions: Economy, Identity and Annexation," in Simon and Tejirian (eds), *The Creation of Iraq, 1914–1921*, p. 56.

5 Quoted in Catherwood, *Churchill's Folly*, p. 201.

6 Quoted in Haj, *The Making of Modern Iraq 1900–1963*, p. 122.

7 Quoted in al-Khalil, *Republic of Fear*, p. 85.

8 Quoted in ibid., p. 81.

9 Quoted in Hashim, "Saddam Husayn and Civil–Military Relations in Iraq," p. 17.

10 Marr, *The Modern History of Iraq*, p. 289.

11 Ibid., p. 274.

12 Quoted in al-Khalil, *Republic of Fear*, p. 206.

13 Quoted in ibid., p. 52.

14 Details can be found in Makiya, *Cruelty and Silence*, p. 287.

15 Quoted in Zaher, "Political Developments in Iraq 1963–1980," in CARDRI, *Saddam's Iraq*, p. 49.

2 Dictatorship and war

1 Quoted in Jaza'iri, "Ba'athist Ideology and Practice," in Hazelton (ed.), *Iraq Since the Gulf War*, p. 42.

2 Zubaida, "Democracy, Iraq and the Middle East," p. 4.

3 Quoted in Khafaji, "War as a Vehicle for the Rise and Demise of a State-Controlled Society," p. 32.

4 Quoted in Jaza'iri, "Ba'athist Ideology and Practice," p. 43.

5 Ibid., p. 47.

6 Ba'athist vulgarity can, at times, be quite breathtaking. During the classical age of Islam such brilliant philosophers as ibn Sina or Avicenna argued that the existence of God was a necessity since the universe could not function without such a being. Hence he used the term "Necessary Being" for God.

7 Significantly, these referendums were referred to as *bay'a*, meaning a declaration of allegiance. It harkens back to the days of the old Baghdad Caliphate when the caliph, seated on his throne, would receive the *bay'a* from the assembled notables. The ceremony was designed to highlight ties of patronage and subservience to the caliph rather than mutual obligation.

8 Quoted in Mohsen, "Cultural Totalitarianism," in Hazelton (ed.), *Iraq Since the Gulf War*, p. 12.

9 Quoted in Pipes, "A Border Adrift: Origins of the Conflict," in Tahir-Kheli and Ayubi (eds), *The Iran–Iraq War*, p. 11.

10 Quoted in Gause, "Iraq's Decisions to Go to War, 1980 and 1990," p. 66.

11 Quoted in Sakai, "Modernity and Tradition in the Islamic Movements in Iraq," p. 46.

12 Conversation with an Iraqi veteran of the Iran–Iraq war who does not want his name mentioned, March 8, 2006.

13 Polk, *Understanding Iraq*, p. 130.

14 Quoted in al-Khalil, *Republic of Fear*, p.278.

15 Quoted in McDowall, *A Modern History of the Kurds*, p. 358.

16 This, incidentally, points to one of the structural weaknesses of the Iraqi oil industry, the backbone of the entire economy. The fact that the borders of Iraq were drawn with only a narrow outlet to the sea remains a major problem for any government, regardless of its political nature.

17 A small town to the northwest of Baghdad in the so-called "Sunni Triangle."

18 Khafaji, "State Terror and the Degradation of Politics," in Hazelton (ed.), *Iraq Since the Gulf War*, p. 25.

19 Conversation with an Iraqi veteran of the Iran–Iraq war who does not want his name mentioned, March 8, 2006.

20 Quoted in al-Khalil, *Republic of Fear*, p. 284.

21 Ibid.

22 Quoted in Hiro, *Desert Shield to Desert Storm*, p. 49.

3 Imperialism and the crisis of Kuwait

1 Human Rights Watch, "Appendix A: The Ali Hassan al-Majid Tapes," in *Iraq's Crime of Genocide*.

2 Ibid., p. 12.

3 Ibid., pp. 143–4.

4 Quoted by Pilger, "Squeezed to Death".

5 Chaudry, "On the Way to Market," p. 23, fn 12.

6 Quoted in Gause, "Iraq's Decisions to Go to War, 1980 and 1990," p. 59.

7 Quoted in Ibrahim, "Sovereign States and Borders in the Gulf Region: A Historical Perspective," in Ibrahim (ed.), *The Gulf Crisis*, p. 11.

8 Quoted in Alnasrawi, "Oil Dimensions of the Gulf Crisis," in ibid., p. 51.

9 Ibid.

10 Ibid., p. 52.

11 Quoted in Ibrahim, "Sovereign States and Borders in the Gulf Region", in ibid., p. 11.

12 Sifry and Cerf (eds), *The Gulf War Reader*, p. 127.

13 Ibid., p. 130.

14 Kubursi and Mansur, "Oil and the Gulf War," p. 7.

15 Quoted in ibid., p. 8.

16 Quoted in Gause, "Iraq's Decisions to Go to War, 1980 and 1990," p. 60.

17 Ibid.

18 Quoted in Hashim, "Saddam Husayn and Civil–Military Relations in Iraq," p. 10.

19 Quoted in Nakash, *The Shi'is of Iraq*, p. 274.

4 The sanctions regime

1 At the end of 1993, the Iraqi dinar (ID), which had traded at $1 to 0.5 ID, was worth 20,000 ID to the dollar.

2 Quoted in Baram, "The Effects of Iraqi Sanctions," pp. 214–15.

3 See Lake, "Confronting Backlash States."

4 Quoted by Pilger, "Squeezed to Death."

5 Ritter, "Exclusive: Scott Ritter in His Own Words," interview with Massimo Calabresi.

6 Quoted by Pilger, "Squeezed to Death."

7 Quoted by Ismael, "Social Policy in the Arab World," p. 2.

8 Quoted by Pilger, "Squeezed to Death."

9 Ibid.

10 Ibid.

11 Ibid.

12 Bossuyt, *The Adverse Consequences of Economic Sanctions on the Enjoyment of Human Rights*, pp. 18–19.

13 Reported in *al-Mada*, September 23, 2003.

14 Khafaji, "The Myth of Iraqi Exceptionalism," p. 83.

15 Quoted in Hashim, "Saddam Husyan and Civil–Military Relations in Iraq," p. 31.

16 CBS News, *60 Minutes*, May 12, 1996.

17 Though most Kurds are Sunni Muslims, some are followers of the mystical Qadiriyya order, while others tend to follow the Naqshabandiyya order.

18 Quoted by Gunter, "The KDP–PUK Conflict in Northern Iraq," p. 232, fn 23.

19 Ibid., p. 240.

20 An estimated 3,500 people were subjected to such mutilation, mostly on the orders of Saddam's older son 'Uday.

21 After the fall of the regime it again changed its name to Sadr City.

22 Quoted in Pilger, "Squeezed to Death."

23 Quoted in Baram, *Who are the Insurgents?*, p. 7.

24 Throughout Islamic history, the mentioning of the ruler's name, often by calling on God to preserve his health, during the congregational Friday prayers, was considered a symbolic recognition of that ruler's legitimacy.

25 Quoted in Cole, "The United States and Shi'ite Religious Factions in Post-Ba'thist Iraq," p. 552.

26 Bossuyt, *The Adverse Consequences of Economic Sanctions on the Enjoyment of Human Rights*, p. 15.

5 Occupation and chaos

1 Quoted in Anderson, "American Viceroy," p. 62.

2 Ibid.

3 The American case for military action was best laid out by then Secretary of State Colin Powell in a speech before the United Nations. He later admitted that none of it was true and apologized for misleading the public.

4 *Washington Post*, November 9, 2002.

5 Yaphe, "War and Occupation in Iraq," p. 393.

6 Weapons were readily available at cheap prices in almost every market area. In one market in downtown Baghdad, a grocer had, next to his baskets of eggplants and tomatoes, a basket of hand-grenades with the sign, "Solve your problem for 2500 dinars." This was slightly more than one US dollar.

7 Quoted in International Crisis Group, *The Next Iraqi War?*, p. 9.

8 Quoted in Baram, *Who are the Insurgents?*, p. 4.

9 Quoted in Polk, *Understanding Iraq*, p. 180.

10 Quoted in Zangana, "Colonial Feminists from Washington to Baghdad," p. 2.

11 Klein, "Baghdad Year Zero: Pillaging Iraq in Pursuit of a Neocon Utopia."

12 Quoted in Zangana, "Colonial Feminists from Washington to Baghdad," p. 22.

13 Quoted in UNICEF Report, *The Situation of Children in Iraq.*

14 Al-Ali, "The IMF and the Future of Iraq."

15 Quoted in Henderson, *The Coalition Provisional Authority's Experience with Economic Reconstruction in Iraq*, p. 13.

16 Quoted in Jamail, *Bechtel's Dry Run*, p. 3.

17 Ibid.

18 As of this writing, the average price of crude oil is running over $70 per barrel.

19 Quoted in Henderson, *The Coalition Provisional Authority's Experience with Economic Reconstruction in Iraq*, p. 7.

20 Quoted by Cole, "The United States and Shi'ite Religious Factions in Post-Ba'athist Iraq," p. 559.

21 Quoted in Wilcke, "Castles Built of Sand: US Governance and Exit Strategies in Iraq."

22 Quoted in International Crisis Group, *The Next Iraqi War?*, p. 24.

23 Quoted in ibid., p. 25.

24 Quoted in ibid., p. 27.

25 Ibid., p. i.

26 Ibid., p. 15.

Epilogue

1 Kramer, *Cradle of Civilization*, p. 157.

Sources

Abdullah, T. A. J., *A Short History of Iraq: From 636 to the Present* (London, 2003).

Al-Ali, Z., "The IMF and the Future of Iraq," *Middle East Report Online*, <www.merip.org/mero/mero120704.html>.

Alnasrawi, A., "Oil Dimensions of the Gulf Crisis," in I. Ibrahim (ed.), *The Gulf Crisis: Background and Consequences* (Washington, DC, 1992).

Anderson, J. L., "American Viceroy: Zalmay Khalilzad's Mission," *The New Yorker*, December 19, 2005, pp. 54–65.

Arnove, A. (ed.), *Iraq Under Siege: The Deadly Impact of Sanctions and War* (London, 2000).

Baram, A., *Between Impediment and Advantage: Saddam's Iraq*, Special Report no. 34 (United States Institute for Peace, June 1998).

— "The Effects of Iraqi Sanctions: Statistical Pitfalls and Responsibility," *Middle East Journal*, Vol. 54, no. 2 (Spring 2000), pp. 194–223.

— *Who are the Insurgents? Sunni Arab Rebels in Iraq*, Special Report no. 134 (United States Institute for Peace, April 2005).

Bartu, B., "Muqtarahat li-Ta'dil Ba'dh Siyagh al-Dustur," *Mawsu'at al-Nahrayn*, February 12, 2005.

Batatu, H., *The Old Social Classes and the Revolutionary Movements of Iraq: A Study of Iraq's Old Landed and Commercial Classes, and of Its Communists, Ba'thists and Free Officers* (Princeton, NJ, 1978).

Bossuyt, M., *The Adverse Consequences of Economic Sanctions on the Enjoyment of Human Rights*, Working Paper E/CN.4/Sub.2/2000/33 (United Nations Economic and Social Council, June 21, 2000).

CARDRI, *Saddam's Iraq: Revolution or Reaction?* (London, 1986).

Catherwood, C., *Churchill's Folly: How Winston Churchill Created Modern Iraq* (New York, 2004).

Chaudhry, K., "On the Way to Market, Economic Liberalization and Iraq's Invasion of Kuwait," *Middle East Report* (May–June 1991), pp. 14–23.

Cole, J., "The United States and Shi'ite Religious Factions in Post-Ba'thist Iraq", *Middle East Journal*, Vol. 57, no. 4 (Fall 2003), pp. 543–66.

Dodge, T., *Inventing Iraq: The Failure of Nation-Building and a History Denied* (New York, 2003).

Farouk-Sluglett, M. and P. Sluglett, *Iraq Since 1958: From Revolution to Dictatorship* (New York, 2001).

Gause III, F. G., "Iraq's Decisions to Go to War, 1980 and 1990," *Middle East Journal*, Vol. 56, no. 1 (Winter 2002), pp. 47–70.

Graham-Brown, S., *Sanctioning Saddam: The Politics of Intervention in Iraq* (London, 1999).

Gunter, M. M., "The KDP–PUK Conflict in Northern Iraq," *Middle East Journal*, Vol. 50, no. 2 (Spring 1996), pp. 225–41.

Haj, S., *The Making of Modern Iraq 1900–1963: Capital, Power and Ideology* (Albany, NY, 1997).

Harriman, E., "Where Has All the Money Gone?," *London Review of Books*, Vol. 27, no. 13, July 7, 2005.

Hashim, A., "Saddam Husyan and Civil–Military Relations in Iraq: The Quest for Legitimacy and Power," *Middle East Journal*, Vol. 57, no. 1 (Winter 2003), pp. 9–41.

Hazelton, F. (ed.), *Iraq Since the Gulf War: Prospects for Democracy* (London, 1994).

Henderson, A. E., *The Coalition Provisional Authority's Experience with Economic Reconstruction in Iraq*, Special Report no. 138 (United States Institute for Peace, April 2005).

Hiro, D., *Desert Shield to Desert Storm: The Second Gulf War* (New York, 1992).

Human Rights Watch, *Iraq's Crime of Genocide: The Anfal Campaign Against the Kurds* (New Haven, CT, 1994).

Ibrahim, I. (ed.), *The Gulf Crisis: Background and Consequences* (Washington, DC, 1992).

International Crisis Group, *The Next Iraqi War? Sectarianism and Civil Conflict*, Middle East Report no. 52 (Amman, Baghdad, and Brussels, February 27, 2006).

Ismael, S., "Social Policy in the Arab World: Iraq as a Case Study," *Arab Studies Quarterly* (Fall 2003), pp. 1–15.

Ismael, T., *Iran and Iraq: Roots of Conflict* (Syracuse, NY, 1982).

Jabar, F. A., *Tribes and Power: Nationalism and Ethnicity in the Middle East* (London, 2003).

Jamail, D., *Bechtel's Dry Run: Iraqis Suffer Water Crisis*, Special Report (Public Citizen's Water for All Campaign, April 2004).

Jawad, S. N., "al-Wadh' al-'Iraqi 'Ashiyat al'Harb," in *Ihtilal al-'Iraq wa Tada'iyatahu 'Arabiyan wa Iqlimiyan wa Duwaliyan* (Beirut, 2005), pp. 213–27.

Khafaji, I., "The Myth of Iraqi Exceptionalism," *Middle East Policy*, Vol. 7 (October 2000).

— "War as a Vehicle for the Rise and Demise of a State-Controlled Society," in S. Heydemann (ed.), *War, Institutions, and Social Change in the Middle East* (Berkeley, CA, 2000).

Khalil, S. al- (Kan'an Makiyya), *Republic of Fear: The Politics of Modern Iraq* (Berkeley, CA, 1989).

Klein, N., "Baghdad Year Zero: Pillaging Iraq in Pursuit of a Neocon Utopia," *Harper's Magazine* (September 2004).

Kramer, S. M., *Cradle of Civilization* (New York, 1971).

Kubursi, A. A. and S. Mansur, "Oil and the Gulf War: An 'American Century' or a 'New World Order,'" *Arab Studies Quarterly*, Vol. 15, no. 4 (Fall 1993), pp. 1–17.

Lake, A., "Confronting Backlash States," *Foreign Policy*, Vol. 73, no. 2 (March/April 1994).

McDowall, D., *A Modern History of the Kurds* (London, 2000).

Makiya, K., *Cruelty and Silence: War, Tyranny, Uprising and the Arab World* (London, 1993).

— *The Monument: Art and Vulgarity in Saddam Hussein's Iraq* (London, 2003).

Marr, P., *The Modern History of Iraq* (Boulder, CO, 1985).

Nakash, Y., *The Shi'is of Iraq* (Princeton, NJ, 1994).

Nu'man, 'I., "al-'Iraq 'Ala Muftaraq al-Ta'adud wa al-Tawwahud," in *Ihtilal al-'Iraq wa Tada'iyatahu 'Arabiyan wa Iqlimiyan wa Duwaliyan* (Beirut, 2005), pp. 545–54.

Pilger, J., "Squeezed to Death," *Guardian*, March 4, 2000.

Polk, W. R., *Understanding Iraq: The Whole Sweep of Iraqi History from Genghis Khan's Mongols to the Ottoman Turks to the British Mandate to the American Occupation* (New York, 2005).

Ritter, S., "Exclusive: Scott Ritter in His Own Words," interview with Massimo Calabresi, *Time*, September 14, 2002.

Sakai, K., "Modernity and Tradition in the Islamic Movements in Iraq: Continuity and Discontinuity in the Role of the *Ulama*," *Arab Studies Quarterly*, Vol. 23, no. 1 (Winter 2001), pp. 37–53.

Sha'ban, 'A.-M., "al-Dustur wa Nizam al-Hukm," in *Ihtilal al-'Iraq wa Tada'iyatahu 'Arabiyan wa Iqlimiyan wa Duwaliyan* (Beirut, 2005), pp. 499–544.

Sifry, M. and C. Cerf (eds), *The Gulf War Reader: History, Documents, Opinions* (New York, 1991).

Simon, R. S. and E. H. Tejirian (eds), *The Creation of Iraq, 1914–1921* (New York, 2004).

Tahir-Kheli, S. and S. Ayubi (eds), *The Iran–Iraq War: New Weapons, Old Conflicts* (New York, 1983).

Tripp, C., *A History of Iraq* (London, 2002).

UNICEF, *The Situation of Children in Iraq: An Assessment Based on the United Nations Convention on the Rights of the Child*, Report (March 2003).

Wilcke, C., "Castles Built of Sand: US Governance and Exit Strategies in Iraq," *Middle East Report Online*, April 8, 2005, <www.merip.org/mer/mer232/wilcke.html>.

Yaphe, J. S., "War and Occupation in Iraq: What Went Right? What Could Go Wrong?," *Middle East Journal*, Vol. 57, no. 3 (Summer 2003), pp. 381–99.

Zangana, H., "Colonial Feminists from Washington to Baghdad: 'Women for a Free Iraq' as a Case Study," unpublished paper delivered at the Inaugural Conference of the International Association of Contemporary Iraqi Studies, London, September 2–4, 2005.

Zubaida, S., "Democracy, Iraq and the Middle East," *Open Democracy*, November 18, 2005.

Index